Keto Copycat Recipes

An Easy Step-by-Step Guide for Making Your Favorite Tasty Keto Restaurant's Dishes at Home, With Healthy Recipes to Lose Weight on the Ketogenic Diet

Lisa Ramsey

Table of Contents

Introduction

Dieting is a struggle for many. When one begins a diet, there is a lot of emphasis on what you can't have, which automatically sets you up for failure. When you have to keep reminding yourself what you aren't allowed to consume it just makes you want those things even more. Going out to eat becomes a frustrating occurrence as you look over the menu and begin checking off all the items you can't order because of your diet.

Those on the keto diet know this scenario all too well. Your favorite menu items are now off limits. You can't conveniently drive up to a drive-thru and order something quick while you are rushing to work or stop by to pick up an order from your favorite restaurant. You avoid going out to eat because sitting down just to order a salad, when you probably can't even have the dressing, isn't as much fun as ordering the steak and potatoes. I remember when I first decided to start on the keto diet. It was a struggle to cut out the carbs and replace them with keto-friendly alternatives. I was clueless about how to make meals and found myself starting and stopping with no success.

After many failed attempts I was about to give up. I wasn't kitchen savvy at the time, and the whole idea of trying to figure out what I could actually cook with was overwhelming, and I would quickly grow tired of the same old broiled chicken and steamed veggies. What was even more discouraging is I missed those fast-food burgers and sweet treats. But the Keto diet doesn't have to be and should not be all bland foods and salads.

After a great deal of researching and experimenting, I was able to successfully understand how I could recreate my favorite restaurant foods from the convenience of my own kitchen! This book is designed to give you this understanding. So, you don't have to suffer through boring meals and failed attempts on the keto diet.

While there are guidelines to follow, the keto diet focuses on what you can eat. It encourages you to consume more healthy fats, proteins, and vegetables while also keeping an eye on your carbohydrate intake. It can help you lose weight, improve your heart health, regulate your digestive tract, increase your energy, and so much more.

You don't have to count calories, restrict your portion sizes, or deprive yourself of the foods you love! You can still enjoy your burgers, comfort foods, and even dessert. You just have to learn how to make this diet work for you and be open minded about trying new foods and ingredients.

This book is designed to show you how easy it is to create mouthwatering keto recipes in your own home. You will find recipes from some of the most well-known fast-food places and chain restaurants that cover breakfast, lunch, dinner, and yes, even desserts! What is even better, these recipes not only taste just like what you would typically order, but many taste even better.

Whether you have been on the keto diet for a while and need some more recipes ideas, or you are just starting out, you will find the recipes in this book refreshing and enjoyable. Additionally, all the recipes are super simple to create. You don't need to have any kitchen skills to successfully recreate these meals. You don't have to focus on what you can't have while on the keto diet when you have an arsenal of delicious recipes to try. You will find that just about any meal you used to love, you can still enjoy when you swap in keto-friendly ingredients, which can be easily found at your local grocery store or conveniently ordered online.

If you are tired of not seeing the result you desire while on the keto diet, don't want to feel like your diet is so restrictive, and want to create delicious meals that excite you, then all you have to do is turn the page!

So read this book now and don't forget to let me know what you think with a short review if you enjoy it. Thanks!

Chapter 1: What Is Keto?

The keto diet has gained in popularity over recent years. It has been touted as a quick way to lose weight and improve overall health. While many people have had success on this diet, a greater number have found it ineffective or have had success only to see the weight immediately come back when they stop the diet. There are a number of reasons why you may be considering this diet or may have started but are discouraged because you haven't seen the weight fall off as you had hoped. This chapter will provide you with the general information you need to know to understand exactly how this diet works and how to make it work for you. First, you will understand why cutting back on carbs can promote weight loss; then you will learn what steps to take so you don't have to fail over and over again when trying to lose weight.

The Ketogenic Diet

The ketogenic diet is a high-fat, low-carb diet that is similar to the popular Atkins diet and other low-carb meal plans. On this diet, you swap out carbs and replace them with fats for the most part. It sounds simple enough, but many people think that means they can eat all the bacon they want and enjoy a number of food items that may be low carb but are actually not beneficial to your health. This is the number one reason why many people fail to see the result they desire when starting a keto diet.

The goal of this diet is to shift the body into a natural state of ketosis where the body uses ketones as its main source of fuel as opposed to glucose. Ketosis is achieved when your body begins to use up the fat stored in the body for fuel over the expectation of being fueled through glucose. Glucose is formed from the carbohydrates you consume, specifically simple carbs like sugars and complex carbohydrates like white flours, pasta, grains, and rice. To kick start ketosis, one must drastically reduce the carbs they consume that will be absorbed by the body and increase the healthy fats to supply it with sufficient fuel.

The transition can take up to two weeks to finally occur if you consistently stick to the diet guidelines. Where many people go wrong with this diet is that they stick to the food recommendations for a few days, then have a little "cheat" meal or treat and don't realize they now have to start back at day one. Most people are also simply unaware of how many items they consume that are loaded with hidden sugars and grains.

This is what can make the keto diet challenging. It takes your full commitment, and when individuals hear that, they shrink away. In reality, it is not that difficult to make the switch to this type of diet, but it does take a little more effort at the beginning and more awareness of what you are eating.

Variations of the Keto Diet

1. Targeted keto diet - This type of keto diet is favored by a number of professional athletes. It helps you time when to eat the right carbs at the right time in relation to when you are working out. When you fuel your body in this way, your body learns to quickly use the carbs as fuel in the most efficient way to help you increase your endurance and performance when working out. This type of keto diet is especially beneficial for those who are trying to build more muscles or who are trying to maintain muscle mass.

2. Cyclical keto diet - The cyclical keto diet incorporates what is referred to as refeed days. With this diet plan, you will schedule in days where you slightly increase your carbs and even allow yourself to have what are considered not-as-good-for-you carbs like white flours, pasta, or natural sugars. What this does is provide your body with a slight boost in glucose which provides your body with additional fuel that can help it burn more fat. Typically, you would follow a stricter keto diet plan for five days then allow yourself two refeed days. This, however, is meant to be an additional plan you follow after you have successfully stuck to a standard keto plan. It is also highly recommended that you include regular exercise in your new lifestyle as the exercises are what trigger the body to burn through more of its stored fuel.

3. Standard keto diet - When you hear about the keto diet, it is most likely that people are referring to the standard keto diet. With this approach, your diet consists of a moderate amount of protein and fat with minimal carbs. The standard keto diet consists of 5% of your foods being carbs, 75% of your foods are healthy fats, and the remaining 20% of the food you consume will be proteins. Many individuals find it easier to transition to a standard keto diet and then move into another type of keto diet or incorporate another keto diet into their lifestyle.

4. High-protein keto diet - This is very similar to the standard keto diet. The only difference between the two is that with the high-protein keto diet, your protein will make up 35% of what you eat ,and healthy fats will make up 60% of what you eat. The carb intake remains the same at 5%.

What makes this diet more appealing than most other diets is that you don't have to count calories or restrict the number of calories you consume.

What to Eat?

Seafood: Fatty fish like salmon, tuna, and sardines are encouraged on the keto diet. Not only do they provide you with lean protein, they contain omega-3s that help promote brain and heart health.

Cheese: While a number of dairy products are off limits, cheese is not one of them. Unprocessed cheese such as mozzarella, cheddar, bleu cheese, and cream cheese can be eaten freely. Cheese contains a healthy amount of fats and provides the body with the necessary calcium to strengthen bones.

Avocado: Avocados contain a high amount of fat, which is why they are recommended to only be consumed in moderation on most other diets. The fats in avocado, however, are healthy fats that can benefit the body. On the keto diet, avocado is used in a number of ways, from creating spreads for breadless sandwiches to using the oil for cooking.

Red Meat: All types of red meats are approved on the keto diet. Keep in mind lean meat and grass-fed meats are favored over processed meats like prepackaged deli meats or processed meats.

Poultry: Chicken and turkey are also allowed on the keto diet with no restriction. Again, choosing free-range poultry is encouraged.

Eggs: Eggs contain protein and healthy fats and are a regular staple of the keto diet.

Nonstarchy vegetables: Vegetables can be consumed freely on the keto diet, except for starchy vegetables, like potatoes. You can literally eat as many dark leafy greens and a wide variety of vegetables as you want throughout the day. Since most vegetables contain little-to-no carbs and they also have a low caloric index, eating more vegetables can promote weight loss.

Nuts and seeds: Nuts and seeds can provide you with a good source of healthy fats. They are often added to a number of keto dishes and can be eaten as a snack throughout the day while on the keto diet.

Berries: Most fruits are excluded from the keto diet, but berries like strawberries, blackberries, and raspberries are allowed in low quantities. Blueberries are also OK, but they do have a slightly higher carb level than other berries, so you will need to carefully watch how many you consume.

Herbs and spices: Herb and spices of all varieties are used in keto meals to not only add more flavor but to accommodate for certain ingredients that you would typically find in a recipe but are avoiding while on the keto diet. You will notice the recipes in this book have plenty of spices and herbs on the ingredient list, even the desserts. This is so you get the same flavor from your meals as you would if you were not on the keto diet. Spices and herbs are what can really help you stick with the keto diet as they keep your meals interesting and enticing.

What to Avoid?

The keto diet focuses on reducing the number of carbs you take in. Specifically, it is the carbs that are absorbed by the body that you want to reduce. These carbs, such as those consumed when we eat processed sugars or wheat products, increase glucose levels in the body. If there is an excess amount of glucose in the body, it gets stored away as fat, which is what we are trying to eliminate. This means there are a number of food items you want to avoid and cut out completely when you are on the keto diet.

These items include:

Sugars: This includes sugar drinks like pop, fruit juices, and teas as well as food items like prepackaged snack cakes, candy, ice cream, and processed foods. A majority of prepackaged foods you find on the grocery store shelves contain added sugar, so you will need to learn to carefully look at the ingredient list to identify where these sugar culprits are being snuck in.

Grains and starches: Even grains that are considered healthy like quinoa, whole wheat, or whole grain are avoided when on the keto diet. This is because these starches are converted into glucose once processed by the body.

Beans and legumes: Though a number of beans and legumes provide a variety of vitamins and nutrients, they too are processed and converted into glucose.

Root vegetables: Potatoes and sweet potatoes are starchy vegetables. They contain a high amount of carbohydrates, which is why when you are on the keto diet, these types of vegetables are omitted from meal plans.

Fruits: This is where the keto diet gets a lot of criticism. While most fruits do offer a wide array of beneficial vitamins and nutrients, they are also loaded with a significant amount of sugar. Even though these are natural sugars and considered better for you, they still spike glucose levels and promote storing fat in the body.

Getting Started

If you want to have success with the keto diet, you can begin to take a few steps that will improve your chances of reaching your weight loss goals and really making this diet a long-term lifestyle. Even if you decide that the keto diet isn't for you, the following steps can help you better understand your eating habits and identify where you can make changes to improve your overall health.

Step 1 - Tracking

One of the first things you want to do before you even get started on the keto diet is to begin tracking what you eat and when. This is important because in order to know what changes to your diet you need to make, you need to understand and be honest about what your diet is like now. When tracking, you want to write down everything you consume, both foods and drinks. Write when you eat, how much you ate, and also take note of any emotion you may be feeling. Emotional eating is a real struggle for many to overcome. By making a little note of when you may be eating because of stress, boredom, sadness, or even when you are happy, you can recognize that these are times when you can turn to different and more beneficial coping mechanisms instead of food.

You will want to track what you eat for at least two weeks. By doing this, you can begin to identify patterns to your eating habits and create a plan for how to transition to a keto diet. Even after the first week of tracking, you can begin to implement more keto-friendly foods into your diet to make the transition seamless and easier.

Step 2 - Make small changes.

After you have been tracking what you eat for two weeks, begin to make small changes to your diet. Swap out high-carbs snacks for nuts, seeds, or vegetables. Begin to experiment with more keto-friendly ingredients when you cook, like using different sweeteners or substituting in almond flour, coconut flour, or flaxseed for all-purpose flour. Making small changes is less overwhelming than trying to change everything overnight.

See where you can easily add in more proteins and healthy fats. You will want to begin cutting back on those items you will eventually eliminate from your diet. Sugary drinks are often one of the easiest and most common items that people begin to swap out. Instead of pop, juices, or stopping by your local coffee house for a fancy coffee, drink more water or seltzer and make coffee at home without the added sugars and creamers.

Take it one step at a time. It isn't a race and making one small change each week will often lead to more success in the long run.

Step 3 - Change the way you shop.

When you commit to a keto diet, you will find that going to the grocery store can be a real challenge. A number of products have high amounts of sugars and hidden carbs that will throw you off your meal plan. Begin to understand how to read food labels and how to calculate your net carbs. This will allow you to make better choices when you are shopping and know what you should avoid. When you do go grocery shopping, stick to the perimeter of the store and avoid the middle aisles. Most of the foods on the shelves you're not going to want to buy, but the outer aisles tend to have your fresh produce and lean meats, which is where you will want to get a majority of your food.

Step 4 - Commit.

The keto diet isn't something that you can do once in a while. For your body to enter into its natural state of ketosis, you need to be consistent every single day. Don't let that intimidate you though. Once you get used to swapping out certain foods, the keto diet simply becomes your new way of eating. When you are just beginning, however, it is crucial that you stick with a low-carb meal plan. If you try to sneak in a cheat meal, you can be knocked out of ketosis, and the process will need to begin all over again.

What to Keep in Mind

Before beginning on any new diet, you want to consult with your doctor first. Since the keto diet does restrict carbs, this may not be beneficial for all types of people. It is better to check in with your doctor and go over any health concerns you may have that can make sticking to this diet more of a challenge. Those with diabetes especially should go over your current health before beginning the keto diet. Though the keto diet can help regulate insulin levels and lower glucose level, people with diabetes are at a higher risk developing hypoglycemia, where the blood pressure drops too low, and ketoacidosis. Ketoacidosis occurs when too many ketones build up in the body, which can cause serious health complications. If you have diabetes, you will want to learn how to check your ketone levels to avoid this risk.

Also, the keto diet is not effective for everyone, but those who stick to it consistently will often have more success. Those looking to lose weight on the keto diet should also add a regular exercise routine to their daily activities. Just as you start slow and make small changes with what you eat on the keto diet, you can begin to take this approach to exercise as well. Your diet is only half of the equation if you want to lose weight. You need to be active in order to reach your weight loss goals. Simply add in

10 minutes of cardio a few times a week. When you make this a habit, increase the amount of time you exercise for or add on another day of exercise.

You want to also be aware that when your body makes the transition into ketosis there can be some uncomfortable side effects. Many individuals have stated that they get flu-like symptoms after they have stuck with the diet for a number of weeks. This can include feeling nauseated, having a slight fever, feeling a drop in energy levels, and muscle pains. These symptoms tend to only last a few days, but when they occur, it can be easy to slip up with your eating habits.

Finally, keep in mind that while your main goal for starting the keto diet is to lose weight, you want to think about the more long-term benefits. Adopting better eating habits and a regular exercise routine should become a new way of living. If you quickly go back to your old eating habits after you have reached your goal weight, you will see the weight pile back on. This will make losing the weight again more difficult.

Now that you have a better understanding of how to approach the keto diet, it is time to supply you with some tools for success. The remainder of this book includes a number of keto recipes that are inspired by and copy some of the most popular fast-food and chain restaurant menu items. These recipes will show you that the keto diet doesn't have to be complex or limiting. You can still enjoy delicious, flavorful meals while losing weight. The recipes that follow all have a brief introduction that provides additional tips, personal stories, and suggestions to help you on your keto diet journey.

Chapter 2: Breakfast

When you are trying to lose weight, breakfast is essential. But busy mornings make it so easy to skip this important meal or even more easy to reach for something that is loaded with sugar and carbs. This chapter will introduce you to a number of those grab-and-go breakfasts that you'd usually stop on your way to work to get but without the excess sugar and abundant carbs.

Starbucks Everything Bagel

Many think that making bagels is a complex process, but this recipe makes it easy, quick, and healthy. You can easily make this recipe your own by using any number of herbs or spices.

Serving Size: 1 bagel

Prep Time: 10 minutes

Cook Time: 12 minutes

Nutritional Information:

Calories 160

Carbs 3 g

Fat 12.5 g

Protein 9 g

Ingredients:

- 2 cups almond flour
- 3 cups mozzarella cheese (shredded)
- 3 eggs
- 5 tablespoons cream cheese
- 3 tablespoons everything bagel seasoning
- 1 teaspoon Italian seasoning
- 1 teaspoon baking powder
- 1 teaspoon garlic powder
- 1 teaspoon onion powder

Directions:

1. Begin by preheating your oven to 425 degrees Fahrenheit, then line a baking sheet with parchment paper.

2. Take a medium-sized mixing bowl and combine the almond flour, garlic powder, onion powder, baking soda, and Italian seasoning. Stir everything together until well incorporated, then set to the side.

3. Take a larger microwave-safe mixing bowl and combine the cream cheese and mozzarella cheese. Place the bowl in the microwave for a minute and a half. Remove from the microwave and stir the cheeses together. Place the bowl back in the microwave and microwave for another minute. Stir again and repeat until the cheeses are mixed together thoroughly.

4. Add the flour mixture into the bowl with the cheese mixture. Crack two of the eggs into the mixture as well. Stir everything together until you have a soft dough. If the mixture appears to string, then place the bowl back into the microwave for 30 seconds, then mix again.

5. Once you have a soft dough, divide it into 6 equal portions. Roll each portion out into a short tube, then connect the ends so you have a bagel shape. Place each bagel onto your baking sheet.

6. Take the remaining egg and crack it into a small mixing bowl. Use a fork to beat the egg, then use a baking brush to brush the egg on top of each of your bagel shapes.

7. Sprinkle a little of everything bagel seasoning on top of each bagel. Then place the baking sheet into the oven and bake for 12 minutes. The tops of the bagels should be a nice golden-brown color.

8. Remove from the oven and enjoy!

IHop Bacon Temptation Omelet

This is the ultimate protein-packed breakfast. Simply making the swap of whole milk for heavy cream turns this into a keto breakfast you can enjoy!

Serving Size: 1 omelet

Prep Time: 5 minutes

Cook Time: 15 minutes

Nutritional Information:

Calories 878

Carbs 5g

Fat 89g

Protein 64g

Ingredients:

- 4 eggs
- 6 slices of bacon (cooked, cut into pieces)
- ¼ cup Monterey Jack cheese
- ¼ cup cheddar cheese (shredded)
- 2 tablespoons heavy cream

Directions:

1. Place a large skillet on your stove and turn the temperature to medium heat to let the skillet get nice and hot. Place a small pot/saucepan on the stove as well, turn the heat to medium.

2. In the small saucepan, add the cheddar cheese and 1 tablespoon of heavy cream. Stir continuously until the mixture is smooth, then lower the heat and stir until the sauce begins to thicken slightly.

3. As the sauce is simmering on low heat, take a medium-sized mixing bowl and crack the four eggs into it. Beat the eggs with a fork and add in the remaining tablespoon of heavy cream as well as half the cooked bacon pieces.

4. Pour your egg mixture into your preheated skillet, lower the temperature to medium low, and allow to cook for 3 minutes. Once the eggs have firmed up a bit, take your cheese sauce and pour it over half of the eggs. Sprinkle some of the bacon pieces on top of the cheese sauce (leave a small amount of the bacon pieces to top the omelet with). Top the bacon pieces with half the Monterey Jack cheese.

5. Carefully fold the half of the eggs over on top of the cheese and bacon so that you have a half-moon egg shape in your skillet. Let it cook for another minute so the Monterey Jack cheese begins to melt.

6. Turn the heat off and transfer your omelet to a plate. Top the omelet with the remaining bacon and Monterey Jack cheese.

McDonald's McGriddle Bacon Sandwich

The sweet and salty combination of a McGriddle is nicely replicated in this recipe. You can easily make one batch and have breakfast planned out for the week. The best thing about this recipe? You won't have to wait in a drive-thru line to get one.

Serving Size: 1 sandwich

Prep Time: 10 minutes

Cook Time: 25 minutes

Nutritional Information:

Calories 279

Carbs 1g

Fat 22g

Protein 20g

Ingredients:

- 6 bacon slices
- 6 eggs
- 6 slices cheddar cheese
- ½ teaspoon Himalayan sea salt
- ½ teaspoon black pepper

For the Buns:

- 3 eggs
- 1 cup almond flour
- 2 teaspoons baking powder
- 1 ½ teaspoon erythritol (sweetener)
- ½ teaspoon liquid stevia
- 1 ½ teaspoon vanilla extract

- 1 teaspoon maple extract
- 3 ounces cream cheese

Directions:

1. Begin by preheating the oven to 350 degrees Fahrenheit.

2. As the oven preheats, prepare the buns by combining the eggs, almond flour, baking powder, erythritol, liquid stevia, vanilla extract, maple extract, and cream cheese in a blender. Pulse the ingredients for about 2 minutes until you have a smooth texture.

3. Next, you will need 12 mason jar lids or a whoopie pie pan. Take a baking sheet and line it with foil or spray with cooking spray, use olive oil to grease the inside of the mason jar lids, then arrange them onto the baking sheet. Fill each of the rings with about three tablespoons of the bun batter. Place the baking sheet into the preheated oven and allow the buns to bake for 15 minutes. The buns will be a light golden-brown color when they are done.

4. As the buns are baking, prepare your sandwich filling. Take a large frying pan, place it on your stovetop, and turn the heat to medium high. Allow the pan to heat up, then add your bacon slices. Cook for about 3 minutes on each side or until cooked to your desired crispness. Transfer the bacon to a plate lined with paper towels to catch the excess oil.

5. Drain the bacon grease from your skillet and return the skillet to the stove; turn the heat down to medium low.

6. In a small mixing bowl, crack your eggs and add in the sea salt and pepper. Gently beat the eggs with a fork then pour into the skillet. Fry the eggs for about 3 to 5 minutes on each side or until cooked to your preference. Turn the heat off.

7. Your buns should be done baking by the time your eggs and bacon are done. Allow the buns to cool for 5 minutes before trying to remove from the mason jar lids; use oven mitts to avoid burning your hands while removing the buns.

8. Now, it is time to assemble your sandwiches. Begin with one of the buns, then add on your eggs, bacon, and cheese slice. Top with another bun slice and enjoy.

*You can store leftover sandwiches in the freezer and reheat them in the microwave for an easy grab-and-go breakfast during your busy week. Ensure that the sandwiches are completely cooled before wrapping them individually in parchment paper or foil, then store them in a freezer bag. These sandwiches will stay fresh for up to six months. You can reheat them frozen—just be sure to wrap them in a paper towel before placing them in the microwave.

Cracker Barrel's Hashbrown Casserole

Potato hash browns aren't recommended on the keto diet, but this recipe substitutes cauliflower instead. You get a hearty breakfast that you can serve with eggs, bacon, or both.

Serving Size: ¼ of casserole

Prep Time: 5 minutes

Cook Time: 1 hour

Nutritional Information:

Calories 242

Carbs 6.5g

Fat 20g

Protein 9g

Ingredients:

- 1 ½ cups cauliflower (shredded)
- ½ cup sour cream
- ½ cup cheddar cheese (shredded, divided)
- ½ cup Monterey jack cheese (shredded, divided)
- ¼ cup mayonnaise
- ½ tablespoon onion powder
- ½ tablespoon bouillon powder
- ½ teaspoon Himalayan sea salt

- ½ teaspoon black pepper

Directions:

1. Begin by preheating the oven to 350 degrees Fahrenheit.
2. As the oven preheats, take a large mixing bowl and add ½ cup of the cheddar cheese and ½ cup of the Monterey Jack cheese. Next, add the cauliflower, sour cream, mayonnaise, onion powder, bouillon powder, sea salt, and black pepper. Use a baking spatula to gently mix everything together.
3. Pour the mixture into a greased 8x8 baking dish. Top with the remaining cheddar and Monterey Jack cheese, then place the baking dish into the oven and bake for 1 hour. The dish is done when the top is an irresistible golden-brown color.
4. Remove from the oven and divide into four equal portions.

Starbucks Cranberry Bliss Bars

This recipe includes a very small amount of molasses, which is one of those ingredients that some will argue whether it is keto. Rest assured! First, it is blackstrap molasses, which goes through an additional boiling process that removes excess traces of carbs but still provides you with the flavor. Second, it is such a small amount compared to the serving size that it has little if any effect on your carb intake. With that in mind, you can always take out the molasses and substitute maple extract in its place if you choose.

Serving Size: 1 bar

Prep Time: 10 minutes

Cook Time: 30 minutes

Nutritional Information:

Calories 110

Carbs 3g

Fat 10g

Protein 2g

Ingredients:

- 2 eggs
- 6 tablespoons butter (softened)
- ¼ cup almond flour
- ¼ cup coconut flour
- ¼ cup flax seed (ground)
- 1 cup cranberries (fresh)
- ½ cup erythritol
- ½ teaspoon stevia (pure)
- 1 teaspoon blackstrap molasses (pure)
- 1 teaspoon vanilla extract

- 1 teaspoon orange extract
- 1 teaspoon baking powder
- ¼ teaspoon Himalayan sea salt

For Frosting:

- 1 tablespoon butter (softened)
- 4 ounces cream cheese (softened)
- ½ cup erythritol (powdered)
- ½ tablespoon lemon extract

Directions:

1. Begin by preheating your oven to 350 degrees Fahrenheit and greasing an 8x8 baking dish with butter.
2. Next, take a large mixing bowl and mix the butter and erythritol until well combined.
3. Crack your eggs in a separate small bowl (to ensure you don't get any eggshells), then add them to your butter and sugar mixture. Add in the sea salt, orange extract, vanilla extract, and molasses and mix everything. Next, combine the almond flour, coconut flour, ground flaxseed, and baking powder into the mixture. Stir thoroughly and set to the side.
4. Take your cranberries and add them to a food processor with the stevia. Pulse for about 1 minute. Fold the cranberries into your other mixture then pour into your greased baking dish. Place your dish into the oven and

bake for 30 minutes. The top should be a golden-brown color when done. Remove the dish from the oven to cool.

5. As your bars cool, make the frosting. In a medium-sized mixing bowl combine the butter, cream cheese, powdered erythritol, and lemon extract. Use a hand mixer to beat everything together until you have a fluffy consistency. Use a cake spatula to carefully spread the frosting over top of your bars. You want to do this slowly as the bars are still delicate and can crumble from too much pressure when frosting.

6. After frosting, place the baking dish into your refrigerator and chill for 30 minutes or until bars have cooled completely and are a bit firm.

Starbucks Egg Bites

These copycat egg bites are just as irresistible as the real thing, but they will cost you a lot less. Also, they are packed with protein and healthy fats that will help you refuel and keep you energized throughout your busy mornings.

Serving Size: 1 egg bite

Prep Time: 5 minutes

Cook Time: 20 minutes

Nutritional Information:

Calories 145

Carbs 1g

Fat 12g

Protein 9g

Ingredients:

- cooking spray
- 10 eggs
- ½ cup heavy whipping cream
- 1 cup cheddar cheese (shredded)
- 12 slices of bacon (cooked, crumbled)
- 1 red bell pepper (chopped)
- 1 teaspoon Himalayan sea salt
- 1 teaspoon black pepper

Directions:

1. First, move your oven rack to the lowest setting, preheat the oven to 350 degrees Fahrenheit, then spray a muffin pan with the cooking oil and set to the side.
2. In a blender add the eggs, heavy cream, cheddar cheese, bacon pieces, red bell pepper, sea salt, and black pepper. Blend for a few seconds so that everything is mixed together. Then fill each of your muffin slots ¾ of the way full. Place the muffin tray into the oven on the lowest rack and bake for 20 minutes.

3. Once the muffins have turned a light golden-brown color, remove them from the oven. Allow them to cool for a few minutes before servings.

Cinnabon's Cinnamon Rolls

Cinnamon rolls are one of my favorite breakfast treats. They fill your home with a sweet aroma that just brings a smile to your face. Unfortunately, the all-purpose flour, different sugars, and other ingredients mean it can be challenging to find a recipe that will work with your new lifestyle. Luckily, this recipe will allow you to indulge in these gooey breakfast pastries guilt free.

Serving Size: 1 cinnamon roll

Prep Time: 20 minutes

Cook Time: 15 minutes

Nutritional Information:

Calories 294

Carbs 4g

Fat 28g

Protein 7g

Ingredients:

- 1 egg
- 2 tablespoons butter (melted)
- ½ teaspoon cinnamon
- ½ cup almond flour
- 1 tablespoon coconut flour
- 1 ounce cream cheese
- 1 cup mozzarella cheese (shredded)
- 2 tablespoon erythritol
- 1 teaspoon baking powder
- 1 teaspoon vanilla extract
- ¼ teaspoon Himalayan sea salt

For Filling:

- 3 tablespoons butter (melted)
- 1 ½ teaspoon cinnamon
- 2 tablespoon erythritol

For Topping:

- 4 ounces cream cheese
- 2 tablespoon heavy cream
- 2 tablespoons butter (softened)
- ¼ cup erythritol (powdered)
- ½ teaspoon vanilla extract
- ¼ teaspoon almond extract

Directions:

1. In a small bowl combine 2 tablespoons of melted butter with ½ teaspoon of cinnamon. Mix with a fork, then take 3 small spring-form pans and grease the bottoms and sides with the cinnamon butter. Set to the side until ready.

2. Take a large mixing bowl and add in the almond flour, coconut flour, baking powder, and sea salt. Mis thoroughly, then add the erythritol, vanilla extract, and eggs. Ensure everything is combined, then set to the side.

3. Next, you will need a microwave-safe bowl. Place the cream cheese and shredded mozzarella cheese into the bowl and heat in your microwave for 1 minute. Use a fork to mix together; the cheese should be completely melted.

4. Transfcr the cheese mixture into the flour mixture. Use your hands to mix everything together nicely. This can take some time, usually about 2-3 minutes, until you have a suitable dough.

5. Once a dough has formed, separate into 3 equal portions and set them in the refrigerator for at least 5 minutes to firm up slightly.

6. Preheat the oven to 350 degrees Fahrenheit.

7. As the oven preheats and the dough chills, prepare your filling. Take a small mixing bowl and mix together the melted butter, cinnamon, and erythritol. Set to the side until ready.

8. Take your chilled dough and roll each piece out into a long log shape; they should be no more than a thumb-width thick. Brush each log with your prepared filling mixture; save a little of the filling for later use.

9. Take your spring-form pan and lay the long side along the bottom, creating a spiral shape as you go. Brush the remaining filling mixture over the top of each swirled log and place in the oven. Bake the rolls for 15 minutes or until the tops have just started to turn a light golden brown.

10. As your rolls bake, prepare the topping. In a small mixing bowl, combine the cream cheese, heavy cream, softened butter, powdered erythritol, vanilla extract, and almond extract. Use a hand mixer to beat everything together until you have a smooth texture.

11. Once the rolls are done baking, remove them from the spring-form pans. Spread your topping over each one, cut them in half, and enjoy!

Krispy Kreme Doughnuts

Krispy Kreme doughnuts are known for being light and fluffy and having an irresistible sweet glaze. Unfortunately, they are not at all keto friendly, but this recipe will let you get your doughnut fix without throwing you off your weight loss journey. For this recipe, you will need a doughnut pan as this recipe bakes the doughnuts instead of frying them.

Serving Size: 1 doughnut

Prep Time: 10 minutes

Cook Time: 15 minutes

Nutritional Information:

Calories 171

Carbs 3g

Fat 14g

Protein 7g

Ingredients:

- 2 eggs
- ½ cup almond flour
- 2 tablespoons coconut flour
- ¼ cup vanilla almond milk (unsweetened)
- ¼ cup Swerve sweetener
- ¼ cup protein powder (keto friendly)
- 2 teaspoons baking powder
- 1 teaspoon vanilla extract
- ¼ teaspoon Himalayan sea salt

For Glaze:

- ¼ cup butter
- ¼ cup Swerve sweetener
- 1 teaspoon vanilla extract

Directions:

1. Begin by preheating your oven to 350 degrees Fahrenheit, then spray your doughnut pan with cooking spray and set to the side.

2. Next, take a large mixing bowl and add in your eggs, coconut milk, and vanilla extract. Beat together until the mixture begins to get frothy. Then, add in your almond flour, coconut flour, Swerve sweetener, protein powder, baking powder, and sea salt. Use a hand mixer to beat together all the ingredients until you have a smooth consistency. Your mixture should be dough-like but not as dry.

3. Transfer your dough into a piping bag (or you can use a Ziploc bag and cut one of the corners off). Fill each section of your doughnut pan with the dough about two-thirds of the way full. Then place your pan into the oven and bake for 15 minutes. The doughnuts should turn a light golden-brown color when they have baked all the way through. Remove the pan from the oven when done and allow the doughnuts to cool for at least five minutes before transferring them to a cooling rack.

4. As your doughnuts cool, prepare your glaze. In a small microwave-safe mixing bowl, add the butter, Swerve sweetener, and vanilla extract. Place the bowl in the microwave for 30 seconds, then stir. If the butter does not melt completely or the sweetener has not completely dissolved, place it back in the microwave until everything has been thoroughly incorporated.

5. Once the doughnuts have cooled completely, dip each one into your glaze. Let the glaze settle on the doughnuts for a few minutes before enjoying.

Waffles House Waffles

Waffles are a treat at any time, but with the high carb content and added sugar, many people starting on the keto diet think that these breakfast treats are off limits. This recipe, however, is sugar and gluten free, making it keto approved! You'll need a waffle maker to enjoy these though, but even if you don't have one, you can make this batter and use it as a pancake recipe instead!

Serving Size: 1 waffle

Prep Time: 15 minutes

Cook Time: 25 minutes

Nutritional Information:

Calories 311

Carbs 2.5g

Fat 28g

Protein 8g

Ingredients:

- 5 eggs (separated)
- 3 tablespoons heavy cream
- ½ cup butter
- 4 tablespoons coconut flour
- 4 tablespoon erythritol (granulated)
- 1 teaspoon baking powder
- 2 teaspoon vanilla extract

Directions:

1. First, take a large mixing bowl and add in your egg yolks, coconut flour, granulated erythritol, and baking powder. Whisk everything together then slowly mix in your melted butter. Continue to whisk until you have a smooth consistency, then add in the heavy cream and vanilla extract. Whisk again until everything is well incorporated, set to the side.

2. Take a medium-sized mixing bowl and add in your egg whites. Take a hand mixer and beat the egg whites until they become nice and firm. When the whites are able to hold a peak, they are ready.

3. Use a large spoon to scoop some of the egg whites into the egg yolk mixture. Use a baking spatula to fold in egg whites, then spoon in more; fold and continue until all the egg whites have been combined with the egg yolks. Don't overmix, you want the mixture to maintain some of the light fluffiness from the egg whites.

4. Take your waffle iron and turn it on. Use a spoon to fill the waffle maker and cook for about 5 minutes (cook time may vary depending on your model of waffle maker, double-check the user manual for approximate cook time). When the waffle is golden brown, it is done. Continues until all your waffle batter has been used.

Chapter 3: Lunch

Lunch is time you need to refuel your body with the right sources of energy. For many, these are often something they can order quickly and take back to their desks, so they can get back to work. Most grab-and-go lunch options from chain restaurants and fast-food places are high in carbs. This chapter focuses on putting a keto-twist on some of the most popular grab-and-go lunch choices that you can make with ease in your own home.

Wendy's Apple Pecan Salad With Chicken

This salad is filling and delicious, but apples are a no-no when you are on the keto diet. This rendition of Wendy's healthy lunch salad uses strawberries instead of the apples. You still get the summer-refreshing taste but without being thrown out of your ketosis.

Serving Size: ½ salad

Prep Time: 10 minutes

Cook Time: 10 minutes

Nutritional Information:

Calories 538

Carbs 5g

Fat 46g

Protein 24g

Ingredients:

- 2 tablespoons vegetable oil
- 2 chicken breasts
- 2 cups Romaine lettuce
- 1 cup spinach
- ¼ cup strawberries (sliced)
- ¼ cup cranberries (dried)
- 2 tablespoons pecans (chopped)
- ½ cup bleu cheese crumbles
- ¼ teaspoon parsley (dried)
- ¼ teaspoon garlic powder
- ¼ teaspoon Himalayan sea salt
- ¼ teaspoon black pepper

Directions:

1. Place a medium-sized skillet onto the stove and turn the heat to medium high. Add the oil to the skillet and allow it to get hot.
2. As the skillet is heating up, take a small mixing bowl and add the garlic powder, parsley, sea salt, and black pepper. Stir until well combined.
3. Take each of the chicken breasts and sprinkle on the garlic powder mixture on all sides.

4. Place your seasoned chicken breast into the skillet. Cook the chicken for five minutes then flip and cook for another five minutes. Once the internal temperature of the chicken has reached 165 degrees Fahrenheit, remove from the skillet and allow it to rest on a cutting board.

5. While the chicken is resting, prepare the rest of your salad. In a large salad bowl add the spinach, lettuce, strawberries, and cranberries. Toss everything together with salad spoons. Divide the salad into two equal portions and top each portion with half the pecans and bleu cheese.

6. Slice the chicken breast and place on top of your salad. Serve with your preferred keto-friendly salad dressing.

P.F.Chang's Chicken Lettuce Wraps

These lettuce wraps are my go-to lunch when I know I have a hectic day ahead of me. They are super easy to make ahead of time and quick to put together. The sauce, however, is what really makes these wraps standout.

Serving Size: ⅛ recipe

Prep Time: 10 minutes

Cook Time: 20 minutes

Nutritional Information:

Calories 155

Carbs 5g

Fat 5g

Protein 18g

Ingredients:

- 1 tablespoon avocado oil
- 1 pound chicken (ground)
- 1 head of butter lettuce
- 2 cups shiitake mushrooms (chopped)
- 3 green onions (sliced)
- ½ cup jicama (diced)
- 2 teaspoons onion powder
- ¼ teaspoon Himalayan sea salt
- ¼ teaspoon black pepper

For Sauce:

- 1 tablespoon sesame oil
- 2 cloves of garlic (minced)
- ½ teaspoon ginger (grated)
- ½ tablespoon erythritol (sweetener)
- 3 tablespoons coconut aminos
- 1 tablespoon apple cider vinegar
- 1 tablespoon almond butter

Directions:

1. Begin by making the sauce first. In a medium-sized mixing bowl, combine the sesame oil, minced garlic, grated ginger, erythritol, coconut aminos, apple cider vinegar, and almond butter. Use a whisk to vigorously mix everything together. Cover and store in your refrigerator until ready.

2. Now, take a large skillet and place it on your stove with a tablespoon of avocado oil in it. Turn the heat to medium, so the oil can get nice and hot. When the oil is heated, add in your ground chicken. Use a spatula to break it apart as it cooks. Allow the chicken to cook for 8 minutes or until it has all turned a light brown color.

3. Once the chicken has cooked add in the onion powder, sea salt, and black pepper. Stir everything together then add in the shiitake mushrooms, green onions, and jicama. Stir and cook for 5 minutes.

4. Once the mushrooms have softened, after about 5 minutes, pour your sauce over the top. Let the mixture simmer for 5 minutes then turn off the heat.

5. Take you butter lettuce and carefully remove the leaves. Place a leaf on a plate and spoon a quarter cup of the chicken mixture in the center. Repeat until you have used up the chicken mixture. Serve and enjoy!

In-N-Out Burger

In-N-Out Burger is one of the best chain restaurants you can go to for an amazing burger. This recipe allows you to enjoy the same flavors and simply swaps out the traditional bun with a lettuce wrap. You can also use portobello mushroom caps if you want a sturdier burger.

Serving Size: 1 burger

Prep Time: 10 minutes

Cook Time: 10 minutes

Nutritional Information:

Calories 466

Carbs 5g

Fat 26g

Protein 48.5g

Ingredients:

- 1 ½ pounds lean ground beef
- 5 slices cheddar cheese
- 20 lettuce leaves
- 1 teaspoon Himalayan sea salt
- 1 teaspoon black pepper

*optional toppings:

- tomato slices
- onion slices
- pickle slices

For the Sauce:

- ½ cup mayonnaise
- 1 tablespoon sugar-free ketchup
- 1 teaspoon mustard paste
- 2 tablespoons pickles (diced)
- 2 teaspoon pickle juice
- ½ teaspoon paprika
- ½ teaspoon garlic powder
- ½ teaspoon Himalayan sea salt

Directions:

1. Begin by preparing the sauce. Combine the mayonnaise, sugar-free ketchup, mustard paste, diced pickles and pickle juice, paprika, garlic powder, and sea salt into a medium mixing bowl. Whisk everything together thoroughly, cover the bowl with plastic wrap, and store in the refrigerator until ready.

2. Next, you want to place a griddle pan or grill pan on your stove. Add a little bit of oil or cooking spray to the pan and turn the heat to medium, so it gets nice and hot as you prepare your patties.

3. In a large mixing bowl, add your ground beef, sea salt, and black pepper. Use your hands to mix everything together. Portion out the meat into five equal servings and roll them into a ball form then flatten slightly to form your patties. Place your patties onto your hot griddle and cook for 5 minutes on each side or until they turn a dark brown color.

4. When the burgers are done cooking, turn the heat off the stove and top the patties with your cheddar cheese slices.

5. To assemble your patties, lay two leaves of lettuce down first. Place your burger patty on the lettuce leaf, top with your favorite burger toppings, then take the sauce you prepared early and drizzle it over top. Place another two lettuce leaves on top and enjoy!

Buffalo Wild Wings Spicy Garlic Sauce Chicken Wings

Finding a good wing is challenging on its own. Trying to recreate one of your favorites doesn't have to be though. These wings are sweet and spicy and are great for lunch, as a snack, or when you are hosting a sports party. No one will even know they are eating something keto approved! You can also skip the sauce and simple season with your favorite spice.

Serving Size: ¼ recipe

Prep Time: 10 minutes

Cook Time: 50 minutes

Nutritional Information:

Calories 498

Carbs 4g

Fat 39g

Protein 30g

Ingredients:

- 2 ½ pounds chicken wings
- ½ teaspoon Himalayan sea salt

For Sauce:

- ¼ cup avocado oil
- ½ cup hot sauce
- 2 tablespoons garlic powder
- ¼ teaspoon cayenne pepper
- ½ teaspoon Stevia (liquid)

Directions:

1. Preheat your oven to 400 degrees Fahrenheit.
2. As the oven preheats, dry your wings using a paper towel then place them on a wire rack. Sprinkle them with sea salt and place them in the oven for 45 minutes.

3. After 45 minutes, turn your oven to broil and keep the wings in your oven for an additional 5 minutes, so they become nice and crisp.

4. As your wings bake, prepare the sauce. Combine the avocado oil, hot sauce, garlic powder, cayenne pepper, and liquid stevia in a blender. Blend until you have a smooth mixture then transfer to a large mixing bowl (the bowl needs to be large enough to hold all the wings as well).

5. Once the wings have come out of the oven, transfer them into the bowl with your sauce. Toss the wings so that they all get generously coated.

Chick-Fil-A's Chicken Nuggets

If you have kids and are trying to get them to eat a little healthier along with you, they are going to love these chicken nuggets. They have a nice crispy texture that kids love and that you will too. You can eat these as is or slice them up and place them on top of your favorite salad.

Serving Size: ⅛ recipe

Prep Time: 10 minutes plus 2 hours for chilling

Cook Time: 20 minutes

Nutritional Information:

Calories 261

Carbs 1g

Fat 9.5g

Protein 44.5g

Ingredients:

- 2 eggs
- 2 tablespoons heavy cream
- 1 pound chicken breast (cut into 1-inch pieces)
- 1 ½ cups panko breadcrumbs
- ½ cup pickle juice
- ½ teaspoon garlic powder
- ¼ teaspoon paprika
- ½ teaspoon Himalayan sea salt
- ¼ teaspoon black pepper

Directions:

1. Place your 1-inch cut chicken pieces into a sealable plastic bag. Pour in the pickle juice, seal the bag, and shake to ensure the chicken is well coated with the juice. Place the bag into the refrigerator for 2 hours.
2. When ready, preheat your oven to 425 degrees Fahrenheit. Then, line a baking sheet with parchment paper. Set the baking sheet to the side.

3. Take a medium-sized mixing bowl and combine the panko breadcrumbs, garlic powder, paprika, sea salt, and black pepper. Use a fork to mix everything together, then transfer to a sealable plastic bag and set to the side.

4. Take another medium-sized bowl and crack your eggs into it. Add in the heavy cream and beat together with a fork. Take your chicken pieces out of the refrigerator and transfer into the egg mixture. Make sure each piece gets well coated with the egg mixture.

5. Next, use tongs to transfer the chicken from the egg mixture to the plastic bag with the breadcrumbs. Give the bag a few shakes and gently press the breadcrumbs into the chicken pieces. When the chicken looks evenly coated, remove them from the bag and place then on a roasting rack set on top of your lined baking sheet. Place the chicken into the oven and bake for 20 minutes.

6. Once the chicken is a crispy golden color remove from the oven and serve.

Mellow Mushroom's Pizza Holy Shiitake

Pizza is one of the most missed foods of those who just begin their keto diet, but it doesn't have to be! This copycat recipe is loaded with mushrooms that sit on top of an almond flour and cheese crust. The sauce is the key component that makes this pizza so delicious!

Serving Size: 1 square

Prep Time: 10 minutes

Cook Time: 25 minutes

Nutritional Information:

Calories 219

Carbs 3.5g

Fat 21g

Protein 6g

Ingredients:

- 3 tablespoons truffle oil
- 1 tablespoon butter (melted)
- 3 cups mozzarella cheese
- 4 tablespoons cream cheese
- 1 ½ cups almond flour
- 2 tablespoons baking powder
- 2 tablespoons Swerve sweetener
- 2 egg

Toppings:

- 1 cup mozzarella cheese (shredded)
- 2 cups baby bella mushrooms (sliced thin)
- ¼ cup oyster mushrooms (chopped)

- ¼ cup shiitake mushrooms (sliced)
- 1 sweet onion (diced)

Aioli Sauce:

- ¾ cup mayo
- 3 garlic cloves (minced)
- 3 tablespoons lemon juice
- ½ teaspoon Himalayan sea salt
- ½ teaspoon black pepper

Directions:

1. Begin by preheating your oven to 425 degrees Fahrenheit, then line a baking sheet with parchment paper and set to the side.

2. As the oven preheats, prepare your dough. Take a large, microwave-safe bowl and add in your 3 cups of mozzarella and cream cheese. Place the bowl in the microwave and heat for 1 minute. Stir and heat again for 30 seconds. Keep an eye on the mixture; you just want the cheese to melt and become properly incorporated, not burn.

3. Once the cheese is melted, add in the eggs, almond flour, baking powder, and sweetener. Begin to mix everything together using a fork; it may become easier to just use your hands once a dough begins to form.

4. Transfer the dough to your prepared baking sheet. Flatten the dough so that it stretches across the sheet or makes a rectangular shape. If the dough is too sticky, run your

hands under cool water to help keep the dough from sticking to your fingers.

5. Once the dough is flattened out, use a fork to poke a few holes into the dough. Place the baking sheet into your oven and bake for 8 minutes. After 8 minutes remove your crust from the oven. If there are any bubbles in the crust, use a fork to pop them.

6. Take a small bowl and whisk together your truffle oil and melted butter. Then brush the mixture over the baked crust. Return the crust to the oven and bake for an additional 10 minutes.

7. As the crust continues to bake, prepare your toppings. Place a saucepan on your stove and turn the heat to medium. Add in your onions and sauté them until they turn a golden-brown color. Add your baby bella, shiitake, and oyster mushrooms to the pot. Allow the mushrooms to cook for 3 minutes, then turn off the heat.

8. Once your crust has turned a nice golden-brown color, remove it from the oven. Sprinkle your mozzarella cheese over the top then pour the mushroom mixture over the cheese. Return the pizza to the oven and bake for 3 more minutes or until the cheese has melted. Remove the pizza from the oven and allow it to cool slightly.

9. As the pizza cools, prepare your aioli sauce. Take a small mixing bowl and stir together the mayonnaise, minced garlic cloves, lemon juice, sea salt, and black pepper.

Drizzle your sauce over the pizza then cut into 16 equal squares and serve.

Jimmy John's Unwich

What is great about this copycat recipe is that it doesn't need much tweaking since it is already mostly keto friendly. This is a quick and easy to put together lunch idea that you can make a part of your regular meal plan on the keto diet.

Serving Size: 1 sandwich

Prep Time: 5 minutes

Nutritional Information:

Calories 422

Carbs 4g

Fat 32g

Protein 18g

Ingredients:

- 2 slices turkey breast
- 1 slice provolone cheese
- 2 large iceberg lettuce leaves
- 1 tomato (sliced)
- 1 cucumber (sliced)

- ½ avocado (sliced)
- 1 teaspoon mayonnaise
- 1 teaspoon yellow mustard

Directions:

1. Place your lettuce leaves flat on a plate. Then, layer a slice of your turkey, then provolone, and another slice of turkey. Next, add 3 tomato slices, 5 cucumber slices, and your avocado slices. Top with mayonnaise and mustard.
2. Begin to wrap the lettuce like you would a burrito. Fold in the ends so you have a square/rectangular shape, the start at one of the unfolded ends and begin to roll everything together. Secure with a toothpick or pick up and enjoy!

Wendy's Chili

Chili is just one of those great comfort foods you want to have a go-to recipe for to create on your own. This recipe uses keto-friendly ingredients that taste identical to the chili you stop at the Wendy's drive-through to quickly grab on a cold brisk day. Feel free to top this chili with sour cream, shredded cheddar cheese, or green onion.

Serving Size: ⅛ recipe

Prep Time: 10 minutes

Cook Time: 1 hour 45 minutes

Nutritional Information:

Calories 362

Carbs 3g

Fat 11g

Protein 53g

Ingredients:

- 3 pounds ground beef
- 2 teaspoons erythritol (granulated)
- ⅔ cups celery (diced)
- ½ cup red bell pepper (diced fine)
- ½ cup green bell pepper (diced fine)
- 1 ½ cups yellow bell pepper (diced fine)
- 1 cup tomatoes (diced)
- 1 ½ cups tomato juice
- 1 15-ounce can crushed tomatoes in purée
- 3 tablespoons Worcestershire sauce
- 3 tablespoons chili powder
- 1 teaspoon garlic powder
- 1 teaspoon cumin
- ½ teaspoon oregano (dried)
- 1 teaspoon Himalayan sea salt
- ½ teaspoon black pepper

Directions:

1. Take a large stockpot and place it on your stove; turn the heat to medium high to warm. Add your ground beef into the pot and allow it to cook for about 10 minutes or until it has all properly cooked and is a deep brownish color. Stir the meat regularly to avoid any large clumps of meat from forming. Once the ground beef has cooked, drain the excess oil, leaving about 2 tablespoons in the pot.

2. Add the onions, celery, red, green, and yellow bell pepper, and diced tomatoes. Stir and let the peppers cook for 5 minutes.

3. Next, pour in the tomato juice, crushed tomatoes, and Worcestershire sauce. Stir and allow the liquid to simmer for 3 minutes.

4. Add in the chili powder, garlic powder, cumin, oregano, sea salt, and black pepper to the pot. Stir, reduce the heat to medium, cover, and allow everything to cook for 1 hour.

5. After an hour stir, uncover, and cook for another 30 minutes over medium-low heat.

6. Turn off the heat and allow the chili to sit for about 10 minutes then ladle into bowls, top with your favorite toppings, and enjoy!

Are you enjoying this book? If so, I'd like to hear your thoughts:
please leave a short review on Amazon. Thank you.

Chapter 4: Dinner

Eating out at a nice restaurant is difficult when on the keto diet but not impossible if you stick with salads and steaks. You don't have to go out to enjoy some of your favorite restaurant dishes. The recipes in this chapter will guide you to recreating flavorful dinner options that you and your family will love. Many of the recipes you will find in this chapter can also be used for lunch options any day of the week.

Long John Silver's Batter-Dipped Fish

That golden crust on Long John Silver's will hook you almost every time. When I was younger, we used to wait until just about closing and ask for all the leftover fried bits of dough. With this recipe, I can relive my childhood whenever I like. The batter in this recipe also works well with chicken strips.

Serving Size: ⅙ recipe

Prep Time: 5 minutes

Cook Time: 10 minutes

Nutritional Information:

Calories 559

Carbs 2g

Fat 43g

Protein 37g

Ingredients:

- 4 cups vegetable oil (for frying)
- 2 pounds cod (cut into three-inch pieces)
- 16 ounces club soda
- ¼ cup ground flaxseed
- 2 cups almond flour
- ½ teaspoon paprika
- ½ teaspoon onion salt
- ½ teaspoon baking soda
- ½ teaspoon baking powder
- 1 teaspoon Himalayan sea salt
- ¼ teaspoon black pepper

Directions:

1. First, take a deep frying pan and fill it with the 4 cups of oil. Turn the heat to medium to preheat the oil.
2. As the oil heats, combine the almond flour and ground flaxseed with the paprika, onion salt, baking soda, baking powder, sea salt, and black pepper into a medium-sized mixing bowl. Whisk everything together so it is well incorporated, then add the club soda. Whisk again until the batter has a foamy consistency.

3. Take your cod pieces and dip them into your batter. Ensure that each piece is coated completely then carefully place them into the preheated oil. Do not overcrowd your pan or your fish will not cook evenly. If needed, fry in two batches. Allow the fish to fry for 5 minutes. The fish should have a nice golden color and will begin to float on the oil when done.

4. Remove the fish from the oil using a slotted spoon and transfer them to a plate lined with paper towels to catch the excess oil.

5. Serve with your favorite side!

Olive Garden's Steak Gorgonzola Alfredo

If you need a great romantic dinner recipe, this is your recipe. The steaks are flavorful, and you won't miss the alfredo noodles with the zucchini noodle substitute. This meal is sure to impress and will keep you on track with your weight loss goals.

Serving Size: ¼ recipe

Prep Time: 20 minutes plus 20 minutes chill time

Cook Time: 25 minutes

Nutritional Information:

Calories 413

Carbs 6g

Fat 28g

Protein 30g

Ingredients:

- 1 pound of steak medallions
- 1 tablespoon balsamic vinegar
- ½ teaspoon Himalayan sea salt
- ½ teaspoon black pepper
- 5 zucchinis
- 4 ounces gorgonzola crumbles
- ¼ cup sun-dried tomatoes

For the Sauce

- 2 cups heavy cream
- 1 stick of unsalted butter
- 1 cup parmesan cheese
- 2 cups spinach
- ¼ teaspoon nutmeg
- ¼ teaspoon Himalayan sea salt
- ¼ teaspoon black pepper

Directions:

1. Begin by marinating your steaks. First, sprinkle them with the Himalayan sea salt and black pepper, then place them in a sealable bag. Add the balsamic vinegar to the bag and

seal. Place the steaks in your refrigerator for at least 30 minutes before cooking

2. As the steaks marinate, place a large pot of water on your stovetop and turn the heat to medium high. Then take a spiralizer and create your "fettuccine noodles" using the zucchini. You can also use a vegetable peeler to peel thicker zoodles if you do not have a spiralizer. When done, add them to your boiling pot of water for 3 minutes. Then, drain the water and transfer your zucchini noodles to a plate lined with a paper towel, so the excess water can drain off.

3. Next, take a large skillet and place it on your stove. Turn the heat to medium and allow it to heat up. Remove your steak medallions and place them into the hot skillet. Allow them to cook on each side for about five minutes. The thickness of the steak will determine how long you need to cook the steaks. Steaks that are a little over two inches should reach a medium cook in 5 minutes per side. If you prefer your steak more rare, cook for a shorter amount of time. For those who like a more well-done steak, cook for two minutes longer. Your steaks should have a nice brown color to them when they are done.

4. Once the steaks have reached your desired cook time, remove them from the skillet and place them on a plate, then cover them with aluminum foil to rest. Keep in mind your steaks will still continue to cook even though you have removed them from the skillet.

5. As the steaks rest, you want to make your sauce. Place a medium-sized saucepan on your stove and turn the heat to medium. Add in the butter and heavy cream. Once the butter has begun to melt, add in your spinach. Allow the spinach to cook down; this should only take about 5 minutes. Once the spinach has wilted, add in the parmesan cheese, sea salt, and black pepper. Stir, reduce heat to medium low and allow the sauce to thicken slightly for about 5 minutes.

6. Once the sauce is done, turn off the heat. Transfer your zucchini noodles to a large bowl and pour the sauce over top (leave a little sauce in the saucepan to top your steaks with). Toss the zucchini noodles with the sauce so that everything gets nicely coated. Add in the gorgonzola cheese, but reserve some to top your steaks with during plating. Toss everything one more time.

7. Now it is time to assemble the plate! Place a small portion of the zucchini noodles on your dinner plate, place a steak medallion on top of the noodles, and top with the dried tomatoes, gorgonzola crumbles, and a little drizzle of your leftover sauce.

Chipotle's Chipotle Pork Carnitas

This delectable dish is easy to make and can be used in a number of ways. I like to make this big batch and freeze half of it for a meal later on in the month. To serve, top your favorite southwestern salad with the pulled pork, wrap in large lettuce leaves, or serve with your favorite keto-friendly tortilla!

Serving Size: 1/12 recipe

Prep Time: 5 minutes

Cook Time: 4 hours and 10 minutes

Nutritional Information:

Calories 317

Carbs .5g

Fat 14.5g

Protein 43g

Ingredients:

- 1 cup water
- 2 tablespoons avocado oil
- 4 pounds pork roast
- 1 teaspoon thyme
- 2 teaspoon juniper berries
- 1 teaspoon Himalayan sea salt

- ½ teaspoon black pepper

Directions:

1. Begin by preheating your oven to 300 degrees Fahrenheit.
2. Next, take a Dutch oven pot, place it on your stove, and turn the heat to medium. Add the avocado oil to the pot.
3. As the pot heats, take your pork roast and sprinkle it with the sea salt. Then place the roast into the Dutch oven pot and brown the sides for a minute on each side.
4. Turn the heat off on the stove once the roast has browned. Add the water, thyme, juniper berries, and black pepper to the pot, then cover. Place the pot into your preheated oven and allow the roast to cook for 3 ½ hours. Turn the roast every half hour so that the flavors really penetrate into all areas of the meat.
5. Remove the roast from the oven after 3 ½ hours (keep the oven turned on), allow it to rest for 10 minutes, then use two forks to pull the meat apart. Once all the meat has been pulled, place the pot back into the oven for 30 minutes.
6. Remove the pot and enjoy!

KFC Fried Chicken and Coleslaw

Yes! Even on the keto diet, you can enjoy crispy fried chicken. This meal is great for any night of the week, and the leftovers make great lunches for the next day. If you like your chicken extra crispy, you can add a cup of panko breadcrumbs or crushed pork rinds to your seasoning mixture.

Serving Size: ⅙ recipe

Prep Time: 30 minutes plus 4 hours chill time.

Cook Time: 20 minutes

Nutritional Information:

Calories 376

Carbs 5g

Fat 29g

Protein 17g

Ingredients:

- 8 cups olive oil
- 2 pounds chicken drumsticks
- 1 ½ cups whey protein powder
- 4 tablespoons white vinegar
- 3 tablespoons heavy cream
- 2 cups almond milk (unsweetened)

- 2 eggs

Seasoning:

- 1 teaspoon celery salt
- 1 teaspoon ginger powder
- 2 teaspoon garlic salt
- 4 teaspoons paprika
- ¼ teaspoon oregano (dried)
- ½ teaspoon thyme (dried)
- 1 teaspoon mustard powder
- 1 tablespoon black pepper
- 1 teaspoon Himalayan sea salt

For the Coleslaw:

- ¾ cup mayonnaise
- 2 cup carrots (shredded)
- 3 cups white cabbage (shredded)
- 1 cup purple cabbage (shredded)
- ¼ cup white wine vinegar
- ½ teaspoon garlic powder
- ¼ teaspoon celery salt
- ⅓ cup sour cream
- ½ teaspoon mustard
- ½ teaspoon Himalayan sea salt

Directions:

1. First, prepare your seasoning by mixing all ingredients under the seasoning section in the ingredient list into a small bowl. Divide the mixture in half and set to the side.

2. Next, take a large bowl and pour in the almond milk, white vinegar, heavy cream, and eggs. Whisk everything together thoroughly. Then add in half of the seasoning mixture and whisk until you have a nice smooth mixture.

3. Take your chicken drumsticks and place them into a sealable plastic bag or a large airtight container. Pour in the almond milk mixture and ensure that all the chicken is well coated. Seal the bag or place the lid on your container and place it into your refrigerator for at least 4 hours.

4. When your chicken is done marinating, take a large skillet and pour in the olive oil. Turn the heat to medium high and allow the oil to become hot. This should take about 15 minutes, and the temperature of the oil should be 325 degrees.

5. Once the oil is at the appropriate temperature, take a rimmed plate and spread out the rest of the seasoning onto it. Take your marinated chicken and coat each piece with the seasoning mixture, then carefully place the chicken into the hot oil. Allow each drumstick to cook for 20 minutes; the internal temperature should be 165 degrees Fahrenheit. When your chicken is done, remove

it from the pan and place it on a plate lined with paper towels to catch the excess grease.

6. Serve with a side of coleslaw (see below).

For the Coleslaw:

1. In a large salad bowl or mixing bowl, combine the shredded carrots and white and purple cabbage. Toss everything together and set to the side.

2. Take a smaller mixing bowl and combine the mayonnaise, white wine vinegar, celery salt, sour cream, mustard, and sea salt. Whisk so that everything is thoroughly mixed.

3. Pour your mayonnaise mixture over your cabbage mixture and toss until everything is well coated. Place the bowl, covered, into your refrigerator and chill for 30 minutes before serving.

Longhorn's Parmesan Crusted Chicken With Mashed Potatoes

Potatoes are considered a high-starch vegetable, so instead of traditional mashed potatoes, this recipe is served with a cauliflower mash. You can also use the same seasoning and marinade on salmon steaks for something different.

Serving Size: 1 chicken breast

Prep Time: 20 minutes plus 30 minutes chill time.

Cook Time: 20 minutes

Nutritional Information:

Calories 557

Carbs 10g

Fat 42g

Protein 31g

Ingredients:

- 2 tablespoons avocado oil
- 4 chicken breasts (boneless, skinless)
- 1 cup panko breadcrumbs
- ¾ cup parmesan cheese
- ¾ cup provolone cheese
- ¼ cup heavy cream
- 1 teaspoon onion powder
- 2 teaspoons garlic powder
- 1 teaspoon dill (dried)
- 1 teaspoon parsley (dried)
- 1 teaspoon chives (dried)
- 2 teaspoon Himalayan sea salt
- 2 teaspoon black pepper

For the Marinade:

- ½ cup avocado oil

- 2 garlic cloves (minced)
- 1 teaspoon lemon juice
- 3 tablespoons Worcestershire sauce
- 1 teaspoon white vinegar
- ½ teaspoon black pepper
- ½ cup keto ranch dressing (see recipe in Chapter 8)

Directions:

1. First, you want to prepare your chicken. Take each breast and use a meat tenderizer mallet. I also prefer the old-fashioned way of just using a rolling pin and pounding each breast so they are about ¾" thick. Then season each breast with ½ teaspoon of sea salt and black pepper. Next, take a small mixing bowl to whisk up your marinade. Combine the ½ cup avocado oil, minced garlic cloves, lemon juice, Worcestershire sauce, white vinegar, and keto-friendly ranch dressing. Whisk everything thoroughly. Place your chicken breast into a sealable plastic bag and pour the marinade sauce into the bag. Seal the bag and give it a good shake to ensure all the breasts are nicely coated. Place the bag into your refrigerator for at least 30 minutes.

2. Once the chicken has marinated, place a large skillet on your stovetop with 2 tablespoons of avocado oil in it. Turn the heat to medium to allow the oil to heat up. Remove your chicken from the bag and carefully place them into

the hot skillet. Cook each side of the chicken for 5 minutes then transfer them to a baking dish to rest.

3. As your chicken is resting, preheat your oven to 450 degrees Fahrenheit.

4. Next, you need a small microwave-safe mixing bowl and add your heavy cream, parmesan cheese, provolone cheese, onion powder, dill, parsley, and chives. Mix everything together and then place the bowl into your microwave and heat for 30 seconds. Remove and stir, microwave for another 15 seconds, stir, and repeat until you have a smooth, creamy mixture. Pour this mixture over your chicken breasts and place your baking dish into the oven. Allow the chicken to bake for 5 minutes.

5. While the chicken bakes, take a small bowl and combine the panko breadcrumbs and garlic powder. Stir everything together. Once the chicken has been in the oven for 5 minutes, remove the dish and sprinkle the breadcrumbs over top. Place the dish back in the oven and bake for another 5 minutes or until the breadcrumbs have turned a lovely golden-brown color.

6. Remove from the oven and serve with cauliflower rice (see below).

To Make Cauliflower Rice:

Ingredients:

- 2 tablespoons olive oil
- 1 cauliflower head (should yield 4 cups of "rice")
- ½ teaspoon Himalayan sea salt
- ¼ teaspoon black pepper

Directions:

1. Begin by creating your rice. You can do this by chopping the cauliflower into pieces and then adding them to a food processor and pulsing, or you can use a grater to grate the cauliflower into small rice bits. Once you have rice, sprinkle your sea salt and black pepper over top and gently mix everything together.
2. Take a large skillet and place it on your stove with the olive oil in it. Turn the heat to medium high and allow the oil to get hot.
3. Place your riced cauliflower into the skillet and cook for 5 minutes, stirring occasionally. The cauliflower should be soft and not mushy. Then turn off the heat and enjoy!

Red Lobster's Shrimp Scampi with Cheddar Bay Biscuits

Shrimp scampi is a simple dish to make, and this recipe can be deliciously paired with any number of vegetable noodles or added to a large salad. Red Lobster's cheddar biscuits are truly one of a kind, and everyone I know says they go there just for them. This copycat recipe of the cheddar, fluffy biscuits is a great side for any meal. The best thing about this meal is that it takes little to no time to have something healthy prepared for dinner.

Serving Size: ¼ recipe

Prep Time: 10 minutes

Cook Time: 25 minutes

Nutritional Information:

Calories 591

Carbs 6g

Fat 39g

Protein 45g

Ingredients:

For the Scampi

- 1 ¼ pounds shrimp (peeled, tail removed, deveined)

- 2 garlic cloves (minced)
- 2 scallions (sliced)
- 4 tablespoons butter (unsalted)
- ⅓ cup parmesan cheese (shredded)
- ¼ cup lemon juice
- ¼ cup chardonnay
- ¼ cup parsley (chopped)
- ¼ teaspoon red pepper flakes

For the Biscuits

- 1 ½ cups almond flour
- 2 eggs
- 1 ½ teaspoons garlic powder (separated into 1 and then ½ teaspoon)
- 1 tablespoon baking powder
- ½ cup cheddar cheese (shredded)
- ½ cup sour cream
- 6 tablespoons butter (unsalted, melted, separated into 4 and then 2 tablespoons)
- 1 tablespoon parsley (minced)
- ½ teaspoon Himalayan sea salt

Directions:

1. Place a large skillet on your stove and turn the heat to medium with the butter in it. Allow the skillet to heat up for a few minutes until the butter has melted then add the

garlic. Cook the garlic for 1 minute so that it becomes a light golden color.

2. Take the shrimp and add them to the skillet. Let them cook for 3 minutes. Sprinkle the red pepper flake over the shrimp, flip, and cook for another 3 minutes.

3. Once the shrimp have turned a pink color, pour in the lemon juice and chardonnay. Allow everything to simmer for 2 minutes then turn off the heat.

4. Add the scallion and parsley to the skillet. Stir everything together and top with the parmesan cheese.

5. Serve over top of your favorite vegetable noodles like zucchini or spaghetti squash.

To make the Biscuits:

1. Preheat your oven to 450 degrees Fahrenheit, then grease a muffin pan with oil and set to the side.

2. In a large mixing bowl, add your almond flour, 1 teaspoon garlic, baking powder, and salt. Use a fork to mix everything together, set to the side.

3. In a small bowl, crack your eggs then pour in four tablespoons of the melted butter and the sour cream. Beat the eggs and sour cream until well incorporated, then add to your flour mixture. Stir your ingredients together until you have a smooth batter, then fold in your cheddar cheese.

4. Take your muffin pan and fill each section with the batter. Place your pan into the oven and bake for 10 minutes. The

biscuits should be a light golden color when they are done. Ensure the inside of the biscuits are done by inserting a wooden toothpick into one. If it comes out clean, they are done. If there is batter coated on the toothpick, put them back into the oven for a few more minutes.

5. As the biscuits bake, take a small bowl and add the remaining 2 tablespoons of butter and ½ teaspoon of garlic powder. Stir together until the garlic powder has dissolved then add your parsley. Once the biscuits have been removed from the oven, brush each one with your butter and parsley mixture then serve warm.

P.F.Chang's Beef and Broccoli

The flavors of this rendition of P. F. Chang's popular beef and broccoli dish are incredible. If you haven't tried coconut aminos before, it is about to become a staple in your kitchen. It is a keto-friendly soy sauce alternative that doesn't have all the sugar and preservatives. After you've tried it in this recipe, you are bound to want to use it more.

Serving Size: ¼ recipe

Prep Time: 10 minutes plus 30 minutes of chill time.

Cook Time: 15 minutes

Nutritional Information:

Calories 264

Carbs 3g

Fat 7.5g

Protein 43g

Ingredients:

- 2 tablespoons avocado oil
- 1 pound steak (cut to ¼-inch slices)
- 1 head of broccoli (florets)
- 2 scallions (chopped)
- 2 garlic cloves (minced)
- ¼ teaspoon ginger (dried)
- 2 teaspoons sesame seeds
- 2 tablespoon water

For Marinade:

- 1 tablespoon avocado oil
- 2 tablespoons coconut aminos
- 1 garlic clove (minced)
- ¼ teaspoon ginger (dried)
- 1 teaspoon crushed red pepper
- ¼ teaspoon baking soda
- ½ teaspoon Himalayan sea salt

For Sauce:

- 1 tablespoon fish sauce (low carb)
- 2 tablespoons coconut aminos
- 2 teaspoons sesame oil
- ½ teaspoon black pepper

Directions:

1. First, make the sauce. Take a small mixing bowl and combine the fish sauce, coconut aminos, sesame oil, and ground black pepper. Stir everything together thoroughly then set to the side until ready.

2. Next, prepare the marinade. In another large mixing bowl, combine the avocado oil, coconut aminos, minced garlic, dried ginger, crushed red pepper, baking soda, and sea salt. Whisk everything together thoroughly. Then add the sliced steak into the bowl. Toss the steak around so that it is all well coated then cover and place in the refrigerator for at least 30 minutes.

3. As the meat is marinating, take a microwave-safe bowl and add your broccoli florets with the 2 tablespoons of water. Place the bowl in the microwave and heat on high for 3 minutes, then set to the side.

4. When the meat has been marinated for long enough, take a large skillet and place it on your stove. Turn the heat to medium and add in the avocado oil. Allow the oil to heat for a few minutes then add the minced garlic. Cook the

garlic for 1 minute. Then turn the heat to high and add in your steak pieces. Allow the steak to cook for 2 minutes on each side.

5. Take your broccoli florets and add those to the skillet along with the ginger. Then pour over your sauce and give everything a stir. Reduce heat and allow the sauce to simmer for 5 minutes.

6. Toss in your scallion and sesame then serve!

Outback Steakhouse Charcoal Ribeye

Outback Steakhouse is of course known for its perfectly seared steaks, and the ribeye is one of the most popular steaks on the menu. This recipe makes a few changes without losing the flavors so that you can enjoy this dinner any night of the week.

Serving Size: ⅛ recipe

Prep Time: 5 minutes

Cook Time: 15 minutes

Nutritional Information:

Calories 139

Carbs 2g

Fat 4g

Protein 27g

Ingredients:

- 4 ribeye steaks (cut to 1 ½-inch thick slices, fat trimmed)
- 1 teaspoon turmeric powder
- 2 teaspoons paprika
- 1 teaspoon chili powder
- ½ teaspoon thyme (dried)
- ½ teaspoon garlic powder
- ½ teaspoon onion powder
- ½ teaspoon ground mustard
- ½ teaspoon cumin (ground)
- ½ teaspoon ancho chili pepper (ground)
- ½ teaspoon Himalayan sea salt
- ½ teaspoon black pepper

Directions:

1. Begin by placing a grill pan on your stove or turn your outdoor grill on to medium-high heat. Brush your grill pan or outdoor grill with oil.
2. Next, take a small bowl and combine the turmeric powder, paprika, chili powder, thyme, garlic powder, onion powder, ground mustard, cumin, ancho chili pepper, sea salt, and black pepper. Use a fork to thoroughly mix all the ingredients together.
3. Take each of your steaks and season them generously with your spice mixture on both sides. Then place the steaks

onto your grill. Cook for 5 minutes on each side for a medium-cooked steak. Remove the steaks from the grill when they are at your desired doneness and cover them with foil to rest for 5 minutes.

4. When the steaks have rested, slice the steaks and serve on top of your favorite salad or along with your favorite roasted vegetables.

Chili's BBQ Baby Back Ribs

Ribs are a summer staple where I'm from. We tend to grill them up a few times a month. The key to making your favorite Bar-B-Que dishes keto friendly is to choose the right sauce. Be sure to use a low-carb version with no added sugar. You can omit it from this recipe if you prefer a dry rub rack of ribs.

Serving Size: ⅓ rack of ribs

Prep Time: 10 minutes

Cook Time: 3 hours

Nutritional Information:

Calories 483

Carbs 2.5g

Fat 41g

Protein 24g

Ingredients:

- 2 tablespoons avocado oil (divided)
- 2 racks baby back ribs (remove membrane)
- ½ cup BBQ sauce (low carb)
- 1 teaspoon paprika
- 1 teaspoon garlic powder
- 1 teaspoon onion powder
- 1 teaspoon ground mustard
- ½ teaspoon cinnamon
- ½ teaspoon celery salt
- ½ teaspoon cayenne pepper
- 1 teaspoon Himalayan sea salt
- 1 teaspoon black pepper

Directions:

1. First, turn your oven to 275 degrees Fahrenheit.
2. Next, prepare your seasoning rub by combining the paprika, garlic powder, onion powder, ground mustard, cinnamon, celery salt, cayenne pepper, sea salt, and black pepper in a small mixing bowl. Use a fork to stir everything together.
3. Take your racks of ribs and generously rub your seasoning mix all over them. Leave a little of the seasoning mix aside for later.

4. Place your ribs on a rimmed baking sheet, cover, and seal with aluminum foil. Place the baking sheet into your preheated oven and allow the ribs to cook for 2 ½ hours. You'll be tempted to check on them because the smell will fill your home, but resist the urge to peek at them.

5. After 2 ½ hours, take the baking sheet from the oven and uncover. Sprinkle the leftover seasoning mix over top and pour the BBQ sauce over top. Return the baking sheet into the oven for another 30 minutes.

6. The ribs should be a rich dark-red color when done. After removing them from the oven. allow them to rest for 10 minutes before serving.

Chapter 5: Soups

Soups are one of those comfort foods that make you feel warm inside. This chapter is dedicated to providing you with a more versatile number of soup recipes, so you don't always have to have the same chicken and vegetables while you are working towards a healthier lifestyle. Here, you will learn how to easily create a bowlful of savory and satisfying soup perfect for dinner or lunch.

Pappadeaux's Crawfish Bisque

If you are lucky enough to have access to fresh crawfish, then this is a must-try recipe. Don't be intimidated by the cleaning or shelling process. This bisque utilizes the extra flavor in its rich broth.

Serving Size: ¼ recipe

Prep Time: 15 minutes

Cook Time: 2 hours

Nutritional Information:

Calories 275

Carbs 2.5g

Fat 18g

Protein 25g

Ingredients:

- 4 cups water
- 1 tablespoon olive oil
- 1 ½ pounds of crawfish
- ¼ cup tomatoes (chopped)
- ¼ cup onions (chopped)
- ¼ cup green bell pepper (chopped)
- 1 ½ cups heavy cream
- ½ tablespoon tomato paste
- ½ teaspoon paprika
- ¼ teaspoon cayenne pepper

Directions:

1. Take a large pot filled with water and place it on your stove. Turn the heat to high to bring to a boil. Once the water is boiling, add your crawfish and boil for 15 minutes. Then turn off the heat and allow the crawfish to cool for 15 minutes.

2. Take the crawfish and separate the tail meat, set the shells and heads in a bowl to use for the stock later, and put the meat in a bowl to store in the refrigerator until you are ready for it.

3. Once you have separated the meat from the shells, place a large saucepan on your stove with the olive oil in it and turn the heat to medium heat. Add the heads and shells

from the crawfish to the saucepan along with the cayenne pepper and paprika. Allow everything to sauté over medium heat for 5 minutes. Then, add the water and bring everything to a boil. Once the liquids are boiling, lower the heat to medium low and simmer for 30 minutes.

4. After 30 minutes, strain the liquid from the pan into a medium-sized bowl using a cheesecloth. Discard the shells and heads, then pour the liquid back into the saucepan. Turn the heat to medium low and add in the tomato paste, heavy cream, chopped tomatoes, onions, and green bell peppers. Allow the vegetables to simmer for 1 hour then add in the crawfish meat. Simmer everything for another 15 minutes then serve.

Panera Bread's Broccoli Cheddar Soup

The broccoli and cheddar soup from Panera Bread is probably one of its most popular soups. It's rich and creamy and simply just delicious. This recipe takes inspiration from Panera's soup but simplifies it and makes it keto friendly.

Serving Size: ⅙ recipe

Prep Time: 10 minutes

Cook Time: 25 minutes

Nutritional Information:

Calories 295

Carbs 5g

Fat 24g

Protein 13g

Ingredients:

- 1 tablespoon olive oil
- 3 ½ cups low-sodium chicken or vegetable broth
- ½ cup heavy cream
- 2 cups broccoli (chopped)
- 1 cup carrots (shredded)
- ½ cup white onions (diced fine)
- 4 ounces of cheddar cheese (shredded)
- 4 ounces gouda cheese
- 4 ounces cream cheese
- ¼ teaspoon black pepper

Directions:

1. Get a large saucepan and place it on your stovetop. Add the olive oil to the pan and turn the heat to medium. Allow the pan to heat for a few minutes then add your onions and sauté them for about 5 minutes.
2. Add the cream cheese to the pan and stir frequently to allow the cheese to begin to melt. Slowly pour in the heavy

cream, then add in the gouda and shredded cheddar cheese. Continue to stir for 3 minutes.

3. Add your chopped broccoli to the pan along with the chicken or vegetable broth. Allow the broth to simmer for 5 minutes, then add in the carrots and black pepper. Lower the heat to medium low, cover, and let the soup cook for 10 minutes.

4. After 10 minutes, you can take half the soup and transfer it to a blender. Blend on high until you have a smooth consistency, then transfer back into the pan and stir until everything comes together. This will give you a slightly thicker but smoother soup. If you want a chunkier soup, then just serve hot after it has cooked for 10 minutes in the previous step.

Carrabba's Sausage and Lentil Soup

While lentils are nutritious, they tend to have a higher amount of net carbs, which doesn't make them keto friendly. This recipe takes out the lentils and swaps in eggplant and cauliflower for a great spin-off on the widely known Carrabba's signature sausage and lentil soup.

Serving Size: ⅙ recipe

Prep Time: 10 minutes

Cook Time: 1 hour and 20 minutes

Nutritional Information:

Calories 338

Carbs 4.5g

Fat 26g

Protein 17g

Ingredients:

- 2 tablespoons olive oil
- 1 pound Italian sausage
- 4 cups low-sodium vegetable broth
- 1 cup white onion (diced)
- 1 cup cauliflower (florets, riced)
- ½ cup eggplant (diced small)
- 2 cups tomatoes (diced)
- 3 garlic cloves (minced)
- ½ cup celery (diced)
- ½ cup carrots (diced)
- 2 teaspoons Italian seasoning

Directions:

1. Take a large soup or stock pot and place it on your stove with the 2 tablespoons of olive in it. Turn the heat to medium high and allow the oil to heat up for a few minutes, then add your onions, garlic, celery, and carrots

to the pot. Let the vegetables cook for about 5 minutes, until the onions are translucent.

2. Lower the temperature of your stove to medium and add the Italian sausage to the pot. Let the sausage cook thoroughly for about 10 minutes.

3. Once the sausage is cooked all the way through, pour in the vegetable broth, diced tomatoes, eggplant, and Italian seasoning. Cover the pot, reduce the heat to medium low, and allow everything to simmer for 45 minutes.

4. Add the cauliflower to the pot and cook for another 15 minutes.

5. Serve hot and store leftovers in the refrigerator for up to 5 days.

Applebee's Tomato Basil Soup

Tomato soup is just a classic. While it is quite easy just to reach for a can of the condensed stuff, you will want to reconsider while on keto. Most store-bought canned soups contain high amounts of added sugars and preservatives. This recreation of Applebee's tomato basil soup will show you that making soup from scratch is not just easy, but the resulting product has more flavor and is better for you.

Serving Size: ⅙ recipe

Prep Time: 10 minutes

Cook Time:50 minutes

Nutritional Information:

Calories 180

Carbs 5g

Fat 13g

Protein 10g

Ingredients:

- 1 tablespoon butter (unsalted)
- 4 ounces cream cheese
- 4 tablespoons parmesan cheese (grated)
- 2 cups chicken broth
- 6 tomatoes (skin removed, crushed or use 1 14-ounce can of whole tomatoes)
- ¼ cup red onions (diced fine)
- 1 garlic clove (minced)
- ½ tablespoon basil (dried)
- ½ teaspoon oregano (dried)
- ½ teaspoon Himalayan sea salt
- ¼ teaspoon black pepper

Directions:

1. Place a large soup pot on the stove with the butter in it. Turn the heat to medium to melt the butter.

2. Once butter is melted, add the diced red onions, minced garlic, basil, and oregano. Allow the onions to cook until they become soft, about 5 minutes.

3. Turn the heat to medium low and add in your cream cheese. Use a whisk to break up the cream cheese and eliminate any clumps.

4. Pour in the chicken broth, then add in the tomatoes, parmesan cheese, sea salt, and black pepper. Whisk everything together thoroughly, then cover and allow the soup to simmer for 30 minutes. Stir occasionally.

5. After 30 minutes, remove the lid. Use an immersion blender to purée the soup (you can also use your blender and work in batches, then return the purée back into the pot). Simmer for another 5 minutes then ladle into soup bowls and enjoy.

Chapter 6: Desserts

Dieting doesn't mean you don't get to have dessert. When you go out to eat, you always have a little room for dessert, and when you are cooking at home, this can still be enjoyed. This chapter will introduce you to baking while on the keto diet. You will learn how to make some of the most irresistible desserts that you won't have to feel bad about enjoying.

Chili's Molten Lava Cake

The gooey overflowing fudge-like center and the most delicate cake exterior will make you think you are eating something you shouldn't be while on the keto diet. When you use this recipe there will be nothing to worry about.

Serving Size: 1 cake

Prep Time: 10 minutes

Cook Time: Nutritional Information:

Calories 172

Carbs 3.5g

Fat 14g

Protein 8g

Ingredients:

- 4 eggs
- 6 tablespoons heavy whipping cream
- 6 tablespoons erythritol (sweetener)
- 8 tablespoons cocoa powder (unsweetened)
- 1 teaspoon baking powder
- 2 teaspoons vanilla extract (unsweetened)

Directions:

1. Set your oven to 350 degrees Fahrenheit and grease the inside of four ramekins with butter then set to the side.

2. Nest, take a medium-sized mixing bowl and add the cocoa powder, baking powder, and erythritol. Whisk everything together thoroughly and set to the side.

3. In another medium-sized mixing bowl, crack your eggs and beat them with a fork until frothy. Then add in the vanilla extract and heavy whipping cream. Use a blender to evenly blend together.

4. Combine the egg mixture in the bowl with your cocoa powder. Blend until you have a smooth consistency. Take a spoon and fill your ramekins with the batter. Then, place your ramekins into the oven and bake for 12 minutes. The tops of your cakes should be firm but still moist.

5. Remove the ramekins from the oven and allow them to cool for a few minutes. When ready to serve, place a plate over the top of the ramekin and flip it upside down so that

your cake comes out. You can top each with keto-friendly ice cream, whipped cream, or indulge in them just as they are.

Wendy's Frosty

This is a delicious, keto-friendly version of the irresistible chocolate frosty from Wendy's. You can easily leave out the cocoa powder for a vanilla frosty or add in some frozen strawberries for a strawberry frosty.

Serving Size: ½ recipe

Prep Time: 15 minutes plus 45 minutes of chill time

Nutritional Information:

Calories 169

Carbs 2.5g

Fat 17g

Protein 2g

Ingredients:

- ¾ cup heavy cream
- 2 tablespoons erythritol
- 1 ½ tablespoons cocoa powder (unsweetened)
- ¾ teaspoon vanilla extract

- ⅛ teaspoon Himalayan sea salt

Directions:

1. You will need a large mixing bowl to begin with. Pour in the heavy cream, erythritol, cocoa powder, vanilla extract, and salt. Use a hand mixer to blender all the ingredients together until you have a smooth and thick mixture. You should see stiff peaks begin to form after you have been blending for about 5 minutes.
2. Transfer the mixture into an airtight, sealable bag. Place it in your freezer for at least 45 minutes.
3. Once frozen, cut one end of the bag and squeeze your frosty into a small cup or serving dish with a straw or spoon and enjoy!

Starbucks Lemon Bread

This is a refreshing dessert that tastes just like the scrumptious lemon bread you'll find tempting you at the local store display window. What is even better about this copycat recipe though is its low-carb, low-sugar content makes it a versatile delight. You can enjoy this as a dessert or even grab a slice for breakfast!

Serving Size: 1 slice

Prep Time: 10 minutes

Cook Time: 1 hour

Nutritional Information:

Calories 117

Carbs 1g

Fat 11.5g

Protein 2.5g

Ingredients:

- 6 eggs
- ¾ cup butter (melted)
- 2 tablespoons cream cheese (softened)
- 2 tablespoons heavy whipping cream
- ½ cup coconut flour
- 1 ½ teaspoons baking powder
- ½ cup erythritol (granulated)
- 1 teaspoon vanilla extract
- 2 lemons (zest- reserve 1 teaspoon for glaze)
- 4 teaspoons lemon juice
- ½ teaspoon Himalayan sea salt

For Glaze:

- ½ tablespoon heavy whipping cream (more if needed)
- 2 tablespoons erythritol (granulated)
- 1 teaspoon lemon zest
- 2 teaspoons lemon juice

1. Begin by preheating the oven to 350 degrees Fahrenheit, then take a bread pan and line it with parchment paper and set to the side.

2. As the oven preheats, take a medium-sized mixing bowl and crack the eggs into it. Add in the granulated erythritol, cream cheese, heavy whipping cream, vanilla extract, baking powder, and sea salt. Use a hand mixer to beat everything together.

3. Next, add the melted butter, coconut flour, lemon zest, and juice to the egg mixture. Mix again until well combined. Then, pour the mixture into your bread pan. Place the pan into the oven and bake for 1 hour. When the top is just about to turn golden, it should be done, but double check by inserting a toothpick into the center and seeing if it comes out clean. If there is still batter on the end, allow it to bake for another 5 minutes, until the toothpick comes out clean.

4. As the bread bakes, prepare the glaze. In a medium-sized mixing bowl combine the heavy whipping cream, erythritol, lemon zest, and lemon juice. Use your hand mixer to blend everything together until you have a smooth glaze. If it seems to be too thick, add another small splash of heavy whipping cream until it thins out slightly.

5. Once the bread is done baking, remove it from the oven. Carefully lift it out of the pan, using the parchment paper

to easily free it, and transfer it to a cooling rack. Then, take your glaze and pour it over top. Use a baking spatula to spread the glaze out evenly over top and allow for some of it to drip down the side. Allow the bread to cool enough so the glaze solidifies, then slice and serve.

Cinnabon Cookies

Cinnabon is known for its irresistible cinnamon buns, but they also have a number of other sweet treats that are amazing. Their cookies are just as fluffy as their cinnamon buns. This takes those delicious cookies and transforms them into a keto delight! They are fluffy and chewy, and you won't even miss the ones from Cinnabon.

Serving Size: 1 cookie

Prep Time: 30 minutes plus 40 minutes chill time

Cook Time: 7 minutes

Nutritional Information:

Calories 65

Carbs 2g

Fat 6g

Protein 1.5g

Ingredients:

- 3 tablespoons butter (softened)
- 1 egg white
- ¾ cup almond flour
- 1 tablespoon erythritol (liquid)
- 1 tablespoon Splenda
- ¼ teaspoon baking powder
- ¼ teaspoon xanthan gum
- ¼ teaspoon Himalayan sea salt

For the Filling:

- ½ tablespoon butter
- ½ teaspoon cinnamon
- 2 tablespoons erythritol (granulated)

For the Cream Cheese Frosting:

- 1 tablespoon coconut oil
- 2 tablespoons cream cheese
- ⅛ teaspoon vanilla extract
- 2 tablespoons erythritol (granulated)

Directions:

1. First, prepare your dough by combining the almond flour, Splenda, baking powder, xanthan gum, and sea salt in a medium-sized mixing bowl. Use a fork to stir everything together thoroughly. Then add in the softened butter,

erythritol liquid. and egg whites. Mix everything together until a dough begins to form. This can take a little effort as it will start off looking really dry. You'll be tempted to add extra moisture into it but be patient; the more you stir it, the more dough-like it will become.

2. Once you have a dough, roll it into a log form and cover it with plastic wrap. Place it in the refrigerator for at least 20 minutes.

3. As your dough chills, prepare your filling ingredients. Take a small mixing bowl and combine the cinnamon and the granulated erythritol. Use a fork to stir the two ingredients together. Then take your tablespoon of butter and place it into a microwave-safe bowl. Place it in the microwave for 15 seconds or until completely melted. Set to the side until needed.

4. Once your dough has chilled for 20 minutes, take it out and unwrap it. Lay a piece of parchment paper down on your countertop and roll the dough out into a rectangular shape. Roll it on the thicker side, about ½ inch thick.

5. Take your melted butter and brush it over top of the rolled dough, then sprinkle your cinnamon and sweetener mixture over top.

6. Begin at one end of the dough and roll it over to the other side. The dough may break or crack, which is fine. Once you have rolled the dough, press it together so you form a long square block out of it. Wrap it in plastic wrap again

and place it back into the refrigerator for 20 more minutes.

7. When the 20 minutes is just about up, begin to preheat your oven to 350 degrees Fahrenheit. Then line a baking sheet with parchment paper and set to the side.

8. Remove your dough from the refrigerator and cut it into 8 equal squares. Place them on the lined baking sheet and put them into the oven. Bake the cookies for about 7 minutes. The tops and sides should be a light brown color when they are done. Remove them from the oven and transfer them to a cooling rack. They will feel soft once they first come out of the oven. but once they have set, they will firm up. Allow the cookies to cool for 10 minutes.

9. As the cookies are cooling, prepare your frosting. Take a small microwave-safe mixing bowl and combine your coconut oil and cream cheese. Place the bowl in the microwave for 30 seconds. Take it out of the microwave and stir the mixture together. Next, add in your vanilla extract and granulated erythritol. Whisk together until you have smooth glaze-like frosting.

10. Once the cookies have cooled down, drizzle your cream cheese frosting over top and enjoy!

Cheesecake Factory's Classic Cheesecake

The classic cheesecake from the Cheesecake Factory is absolutely divine. It is everything you want in a cheesecake: rich, creamy, and delicious. Unfortunately, it also includes a number of ingredients that you want to avoid while on the keto diet. This recipe gives you a worthy replacement that is just as indulgent but healthier.

Serving Size: 1/12 cheesecake

Prep Time: 15 minutes plus 24 hours chill time

Cook Time: 1 hour

Nutritional Information:

Calories 348

Carbs 3g

Fat 34g

Protein 8g

Ingredients:

For Crust:

- ¾ cup almond flour
- 3 tablespoons flaxseed (ground)
- 6 tablespoons butter (melted)

- ⅓ cup walnuts (chopped fine)
- ⅓ cup erythritol
- ¼ teaspoon Himalayan sea salt

For Filling:

- 3 eggs
- 1 ½ cups erythritol
- 24 ounces cream cheese (softened)
- 8 ounces sour cream
- 2 teaspoons lemon juice
- 2 teaspoons vanilla extract
- ¼ teaspoon Himalayan sea salt

Directions:

1. Begin by preheating your oven to 375 degrees Fahrenheit.
2. Next, start by making the crust. In a large mixing bowl, stir together the almond flour, ground flax seeds, finely chopped walnuts, and the sea salt.
3. In a small mixing bowl, combine the melted butter and erythritol. Pour the butter mixture into the flour bowl and mix thoroughly. Take a 9-inch spring-form pan and pour your crust into it. Use your hand to evenly spread the dough across the bottom of the pan, pressing gently. Place the pan into your oven and bake for 10 minutes. The crust should turn a light golden color. Remove from the oven and allow it to cool.
4. Lower the temperature of your oven to 325 degrees.

5. As your crust cools, place your cream cheese into a large mixing bowl. Use a hand blender or stand-alone mixer, set to the lowest setting, to beat the cream cheese until it is fluffy. Then add in the erythritol and continue to mix until you have a rich, creamy texture. Now add the eggs one at a time. Next add in the sea salt, lemon juice, and vanilla extract. Beat together until everything is nicely combined then add in the sour cream. Once everything has been mixed thoroughly, pour the mixture over your cooled crust. Then place the pan into the oven and bake for 50 minutes. After 50 minutes, check to see if the top has turned a light golden-brown color. If the top has not started to brown, leave in for another 5-10 minutes. Once the top has turned a light brown, turn off the oven and keep the cheesecake in it for at least an hour with the oven door slightly opened. This will reduce the risk of the cheesecake cracking when it cools too fast.

6. After an hour, remove the pan from the oven and allow it to come to room temperature, then place it in the refrigerator for 24 hours before serving.

Chapter 7: Drinks

While water is the best for you to drink when you are drinking to lose weight, it can get quite boring. This chapter provides you with a number of refreshing and delightful drinks from a number of popular restaurants. These recipes are a great alternative to the juices, pops, and coffees you might be used to reaching for.

Orange Julius's Orange Julius

An Orange Julius is a refreshing drink that is delicious at any time of year. Unfortunately, the orange juice and other citrus juices used in this drink are not keto friendly. This recipe utilizes orange extract and cream cheese to give it the citrus, tangy, and smooth flavors that make the original so delightful. After one sip, you won't believe you aren't drinking the real thing.

Serving Size: ½ recipe

Prep Time: 5 minutes

Nutritional Information:

Calories 325

Carbs 2.5g

Fat 34g

Protein 3g

Ingredients:

- ⅔ cup heavy cream
- 2 tablespoons cream cheese
- 3 tablespoons erythritol
- 1 ½ teaspoons lemon juice
- 1 ½ teaspoons orange extract
- 1 ½ cups crushed ice

Directions:

1. Pour the heavy cream into your blender and blend on high until it begins to thicken.
2. Add in the cream cheese, erythritol, lemon juice, orange extract, and crushed ice. Blend for another minute until the mixture becomes smooth and creamy.
3. Pour into two equal servings and drink away!

McDonald's Shamrock Shake

Each year when McDonald's announces the return of the Shamrock Shake, people flock to the nearest one and go crazy! With this easy to make copycat recipe, you won't have to wait or skip this refreshing treat. The spinach powder is what gives it that recognizable green color, but it also packs a nutritional punch you won't get with the original.

Serving Size: ½ recipe

Prep Time: 5 minutes

Nutritional Information:

Calories 354

Carbs 7g

Fat 31.5g

Protein 3g

Ingredients:

- ¾ cup almond milk (unsweetened)
- ¼ cup low-carb keto vanilla ice cream
- 2 teaspoons spinach powder
- ¼ teaspoon mint extract

Directions:

1. Pour the almond milk into a food processor then add in the ice cream, spinach powder, and mint extract. Secure the lid and pulse for 1 minute until you have a smooth mixture.
2. Pour the shake into two equal portions and enjoy.

Starbucks Coffee Frappuccino

When you want a fancy coffee but want to avoid all the extra milk, creamer, and sugar, this is your recipe. It perfectly mimics Starbucks popular frappuccinos that will cool you down on a warm day any time.

Serving Size: ½ recipe

Prep Time: 5 minutes

Nutritional Information:

Calories 182

Carbs 1g

Fat 15g

Protein 1g

Ingredients:

- ½ cup heavy cream
- ½ cup cold brewed coffee
- ¾ teaspoon erythritol
- 1 ½ cups ice

Directions:

1. Pour the heavy cream, cold-brewed coffee, and erythritol into a blender. Add your ice and pulse for about a minute until you have a thick and smooth mixture.
2. Pour into two equal servings. You can top with keto-friendly whipped cream and low-carb caramel sauce if you desire.

Starbucks Iced Matcha Latte

This recipe is a great option for those who love their green tea. The almond milk and vanilla syrup tone down the bitterness of the matcha powder for a perfectly balanced iced tea.

Serving Size: ½ recipe

Prep Time: 5 minutes

Nutritional Information:

Calories 200

Carbs 4g

Fat 16g

Protein 5g

Ingredients:

- 2 tablespoons avocado oil
- 2 cups almond milk (unsweetened)
- 2 tablespoons vanilla syrup (sugar free)
- 2 teaspoons matcha powder
- 2 cups ice

Directions:

1. Pour the almond milk, avocado oil, and vanilla syrup into the blender, then add the matcha powder. Secure the lid and pulse three times. Uncover, add your ice, and place the lid back on. Pulse for 1 minute until the mixture is nice and smooth.
2. Pour your iced matcha latte into two equal portions and enjoy!

Chapter 8: Sauces and Dressings

Keto-friendly sauces and dressing are hard to find. Even when you come across one in the grocery store that says low carb or no sugar added, there's a good chance these labels are misleading. To avoid consuming something you want to avoid, this recipe will provide you with an array of sauces and dressing.

McDonald's Big Mac Special Sauce

The secret sauce on the McDonald's Big Mac is an infamous sauce that many try to replicate. While most other recipes call for excess sugar, this one gives you the same flavors without unnecessary carbs. Now you'll be able to make your own Big Mac (minus the bun) at home whenever you want!

Serving Size: ⅙ recipe

Prep Time: 5 minutes

Nutritional Information:

Calories 138

Carbs 1g

Fat 16g

Protein 0g

Ingredients:

- ½ cup mayonnaise
- 1 teaspoon erythritol
- 1 teaspoon dill pickle juice
- 1 tablespoon white onion (diced)
- 2 tablespoons pickles (diced)
- 1 tablespoon keto ketchup

Directions:

1. Combine the mayonnaise, erythritol, pickle juice, diced onions, pickles, and keto ketchup into a small mixing bowl. Use a fork or spoon to mix everything together thoroughly. Transfer to an airtight container and store in your refrigerator until ready to use.

Chipotle Sweet and Smoky Vinaigrette

This sweet and spicy dressing is the perfect topping for any salad. You can also drizzle it over roasted vegetables or use it as a marinade for chicken, steaks, or fish.

Serving Size: 1/32 recipe

Prep Time: 5 minutes

Nutritional Information:

Calories 103

Carbs 3g

Fat 11.5g

Protein 1g

Ingredients:

- 1 ½ cups avocado oil
- ½ cup red wine vinegar
- ⅓ cup erythritol (liquid)
- 1 tablespoon adobo sauce
- 1 teaspoon oregano (dried)
- 1 teaspoon garlic powder
- 1 teaspoon cumin
- 1 tablespoon Himalayan sea salt
- 1 ½ tablespoons black pepper
- 1 tablespoon water

Directions:

1. In your food processor, add the red wine vinegar, erythritol, adobo sauce, oregano, garlic powder, cumin, sea salt, black pepper, and water. Secure the lid and pulse for 30 seconds until the mixture is nice and smooth.

2. After 30 seconds of pulsing, slowly pour in the oil as you continue to blend. Once all the oil is added, pulse for another 30 seconds.

3. Transfer the dressing to an airtight container and use as needed.

Olive Garden's Angry Alfredo Sauce

This alfredo sauce adds a little kick to traditional sauces. It has a little bit of spice that isn't overwhelming but will wake up your taste buds. You can easily put this sauce together even on your busiest of days and have a delicious and healthy meal ready in a little over ten minutes (if you are making your own noodles), but it will seem like you spent all day in the kitchen.

Serving Size: ¼ cup

Cook Time: 10 minutes

Nutritional Information:

Calories 345

Carbs 2.2g

Fat 32g

Protein 13.5g

Ingredients:

- 1 cup heavy cream
- ½ cup butter
- ½ cup parmesan cheese
- ¼ teaspoon red pepper flakes
- ½ teaspoon garlic powder

Directions:

1. Place a saucepan on your stove and turn it to medium heat. Add the butter, and when it has melted completely, pour in the heavy cream. Stir the mixture until the cream begins to bubble then add the parmesan cheese. Allow the sauce to thicken, stirring occasionally, this should take about 5 minutes.
2. Lower the heat and add in the red pepper flakes and garlic powder. Stir, and simmer the sauce for another minute. Ladle on top of your favorite veggie noodles and enjoy!

Keto Ketchup

Ketchup is one of the most popular condiments for so many dishes. Store-bought ketchup, unfortunately, is loaded with added sugars and carbs. This recipe allows you to enjoy the traditional flavors of ketchup but cuts out all the extra sugars and uses mushrooms as a thickening instead of the flour or cornstarch many other homemade recipes call for. You can store this ketchup in your refrigerator for up to a month once it has cooled completely and is in an airtight container.

Serving Size: 1 tablespoon

Prep Time: 10 minutes

Cook Time: 45 minutes

Nutritional Information:

Calories 10

Carbs 2.5g

Fat .5g

Protein .5g

Ingredients:

- 3 pounds (around 24) plum tomatoes (quartered)
- ¼ cup mushrooms (diced fine)
- ¼ cup white vinegar
- ¼ teaspoon allspice
- ¼ teaspoon onion powder
- ¼ teaspoon garlic powder
- 2 teaspoons erythritol (granulated)

Directions:

1. Place a large saucepan on your stove and turn the heat to medium.
2. Add the quartered tomatoes, diced mushrooms, vinegar, allspice, onion powder, garlic powder, and erythritol to the saucepan. Give everything a stir, cover, and cook for 30 minutes.
3. After 30 minutes, uncover, transfer to a blender, and blend until you have a smooth consistency. Return the mixture to the saucepan, lower the temperature to

medium low, and simmer for another 10 minutes. Stir occasionally. Then turn off the heat.

4. Allow the ketchup to cool completely. Transfer to an airtight container and use as needed.

Ranch Dressing

Ranch dressing is one of the most popular dressings, but it is typically made with milk and sweeteners that you are trying to cut out of your diet. This recipe gives you the ideal alternative that is tangy and delicious. What's great about this dressing is that you can modify it to satisfy your taste buds. Want your ranch to have more of a dill flavor? Just add a little more.

Serving Size: 1/12 recipe

Prep Time: 5 minutes

Nutritional Information:

Calories 156

Carbs .5g

Fat 16.5g

Protein .5g

Ingredients:

- 1 cup mayonnaise

- ½ cup sour cream
- ¼ cup almond milk (unsweetened)
- 2 teaspoons lemon juice
- 2 teaspoons parsley (dried)
- 1 teaspoon dill (dried)
- 1 teaspoon chives (dried)
- ½ teaspoon garlic powder
- ½ teaspoon onion powder
- ½ teaspoon Himalayan sea salt
- ¼ teaspoon ground black pepper

Directions:

1. In a mason jar or medium mixing bowl, add the mayonnaise, sour cream, lemon juice, parsley, dill, chives, garlic powder, onion powder, sea salt, and black pepper. Whisk everything together.

2. Slowly add in the almond milk. If you want to have a thicker dressing for dipping, add less almond milk. For a thinner dressing for salads, add slightly more almond milk.

3. Cover with a mason jar lid or transfer to an airtight container and store in your refrigerator for up to two weeks.

Conclusion

Dieting does not have to mean deprivation. While the keto diet can be viewed as a restrictive diet, what it really is, is just a new way to approach what you eat. You don't have to dread never getting to enjoy a dessert or your favorite meals you loved ordering when you would go out to eat. You don't have to struggle to come up with exciting meals that will encourage you to stick to your goals.

This book has provided you with a basic understanding of how to transition to a low-carb, high-fat diet. We have discussed the first steps you can take to make the keto diet not just another diet, but a new way of eating. When you first understand where you are starting, you know what direction to go in. The action steps in the first chapter help you achieve just that.

You have been provided with some easy-to-make meals that won't throw you off your weight loss goals. Unlike when I first attempted the keto diet, you are already set up for success! You don't have to go back and forth trying to find the right ingredient to substitute. The recipes in this book do that for you already!

The recipes in this book provide you with the first steps to learning how to cook the right way while on the keto diet. You have been introduced to a number of new ingredients that allow you to still enjoy your favorite meals. These recipes can become your go-to for breakfast on the go and quick lunches, and even your kids will willingly sit down and eat dinner!

Now that you have everything you need to get started and have success on the keto diet, it is up to you to make the commitment and actually take the first step. I encourage you to start today! Create a meal plan that swaps out those unhealthy carbs and introduces more vegetables and lean meats. Choose one breakfast, lunch, and dinner recipe from this book to try this week. Don't be intimidated by the newness of this diet. Don't focus on what you will have to give up because, for the most part, there is almost always a keto-friendly alternative or copycat recipe that will make you realize this diet isn't as restrictive as you may have first believed.

Once you just get started and try new recipes, you will quickly make the keto way of eating a part of your lifestyle. And when you do, you will reap the benefits of a healthier and satisfying life. This is just the first step on your journey to a happier and healthier lifestyle that will continue to give back for years to come. Now it is up to you to just take the first step. Good luck and happy eating!

Did you enjoy this book? Please let me know your thoughts by leaving a short review on Amazon! Thanks again.

References

Baker, K. (2020). Keto copycat recipes: Delicious, quick, healthy, and easy to follow cookbook for making your favorite restaurant dishes at home the ketogenic way. Amazon.com Services LLC.

The easiest keto waffles - award winning recipe - 2.5g net carbs. (n.d.). Ditch the Carbs. www.ditchthecarbs.com/keto-waffles/

Keller, K. (2020) Keto copycat recipes cookbook: Easy, vibrant, and classic restaurant favorites adapted into the low carb, high fat ketogenic diet! Amazon.com Services LLC.

Lauren. (2020, January 1). Keto copycat In N' Out burger. Bonappeteach. www.bonappeteach.com/keto-copycat-in-n-out-burger/#.XQKLQ9NKg6U

Lina. (2019, January 2019). Make your own Jimmy John's Unwich at home! Hip2Keto, hip2keto.com/recipes/keto-copycat-jimmy-johns-unwich-recipe/

Lyndsey. (2018, June 12). Keto donuts recipe {Krispy Kreme copycat}. Momma Fit Lyndsey. www.mommafitlyndsey.com/keto-donuts/

Marley. (2018. December 20). Love Wendy's famous chili? Try our keto copycat recipe! Hip2Keto.

hip2keto.com/recipes/wendys-chili-keto-copycat-recipe/

Mawer, R. (2018, July 30). The ketogenic diet: A detailed beginner's guide to keto. Healthline. www.healthline.com/nutrition/ketogenic-diet-101#17

Maya. (2017, August 21). Low carb keto ranch dressing recipe (quick & easy). Wholesome Yum. www.wholesomeyum.com/recipes/low-carb-keto-ranch-dressing/

Sammysamgurl. (2018, January 31). Cinnabon keto cookies w/ cream cheese frosting. Mouthwatering Motivation. mouthwateringmotivation.com/2018/01/31/cinnabon-keto-cookies-w-cream-cheese-frosting/

Sugar-free instant pot ketchup + video. (n.d.). Ditch the Carbs. www.ditchthecarbs.com/sugar-free-instant-pot-ketchup/

Trenum, K. (2019, March 30). Keto lemon bread recipe: Perfectly moist & delicious. Kasey Trenum. kaseytrenum.com/keto-lemon-bread-recipe-perfectly-moist-delicious/